ELIZABETH GARLAND'S

– ADDRESSES –

Illustrated by
LYS DE BRAY

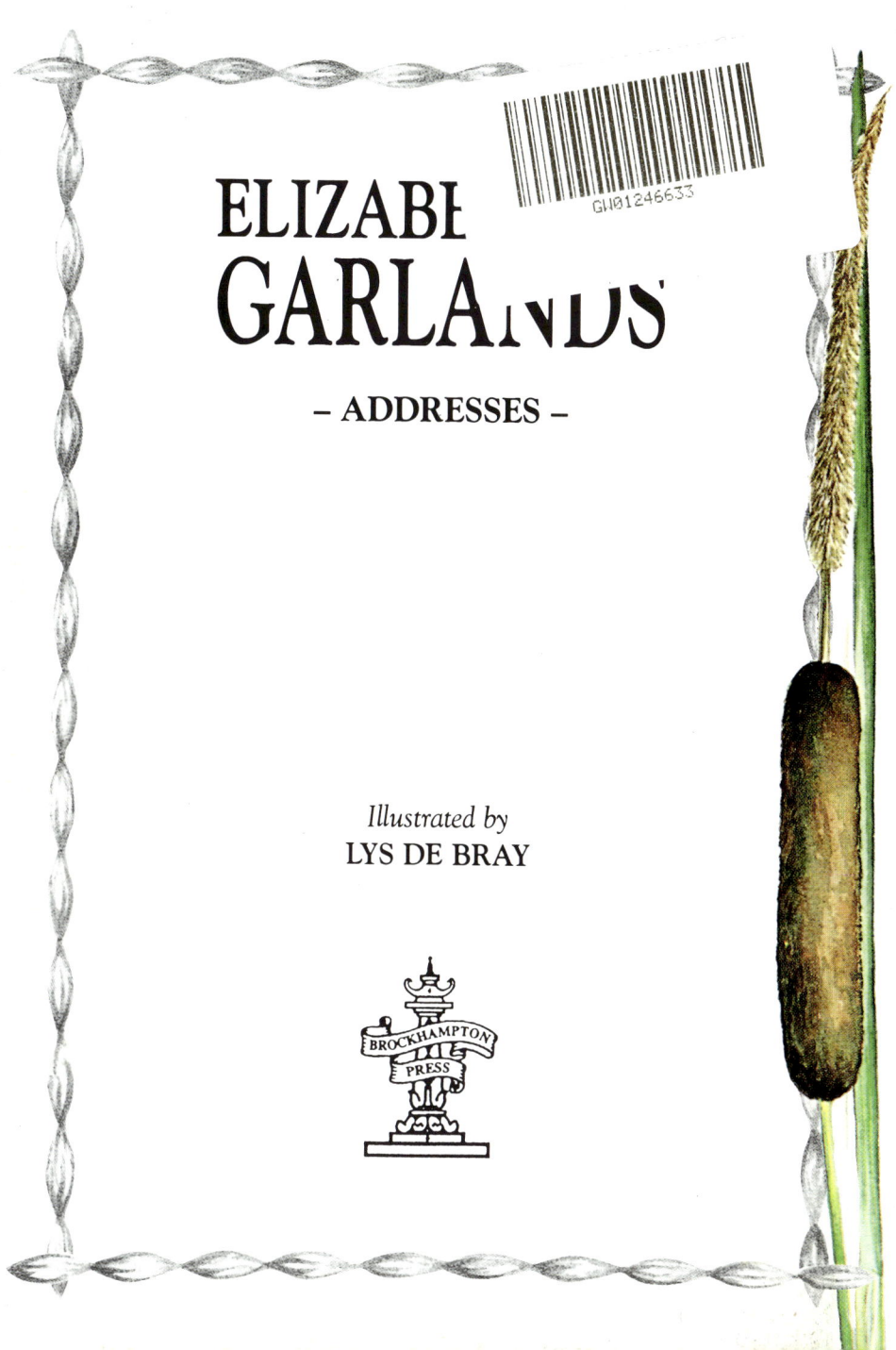

BROCKHAMPTON PRESS

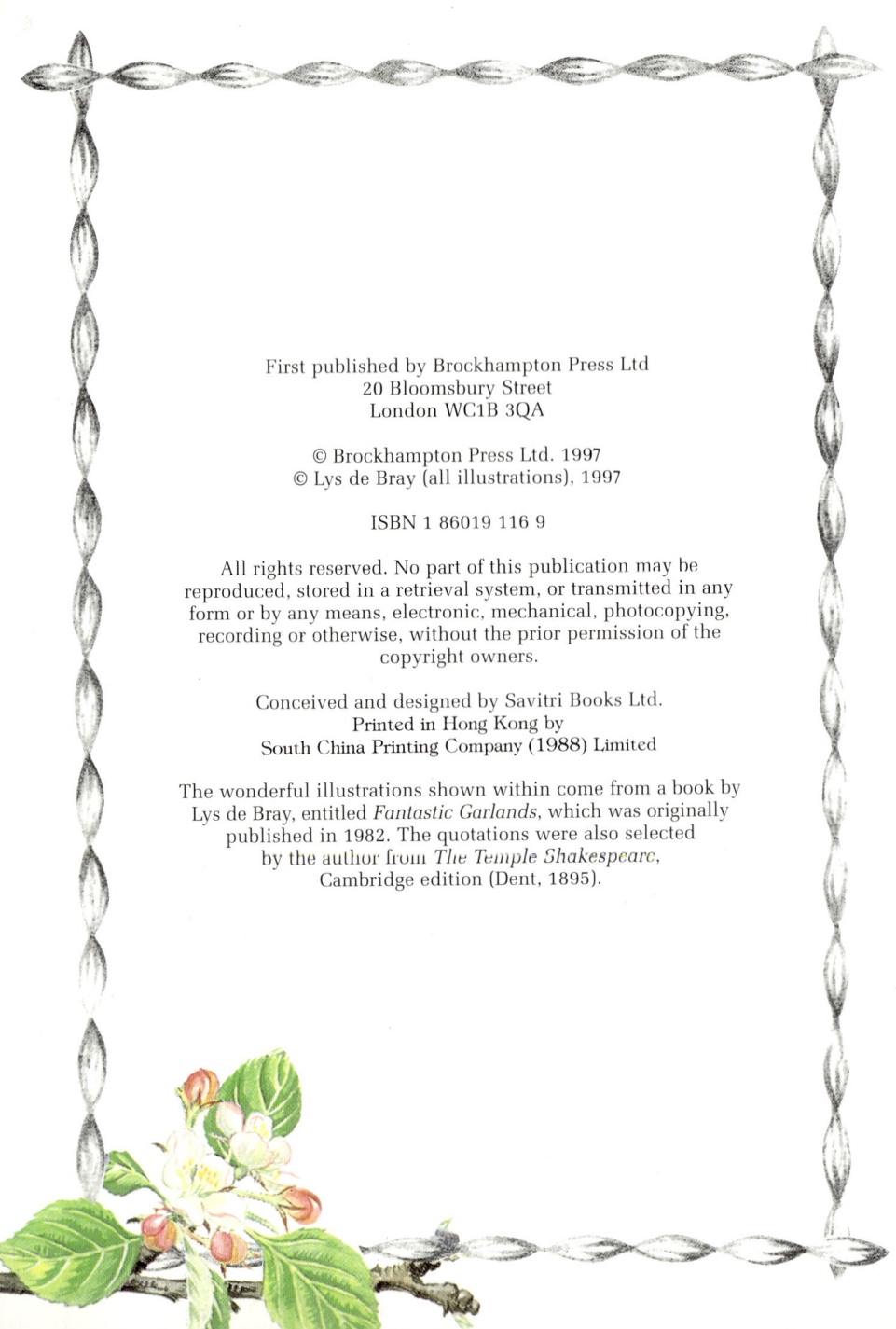

First published by Brockhampton Press Ltd
20 Bloomsbury Street
London WC1B 3QA

© Brockhampton Press Ltd. 1997
© Lys de Bray (all illustrations), 1997

ISBN 1 86019 116 9

All rights reserved. No part of this publication may be reproduced, stored in a retrieval system, or transmitted in any form or by any means, electronic, mechanical, photocopying, recording or otherwise, without the prior permission of the copyright owners.

Conceived and designed by Savitri Books Ltd.
Printed in Hong Kong by
South China Printing Company (1988) Limited

The wonderful illustrations shown within come from a book by Lys de Bray, entitled *Fantastic Garlands*, which was originally published in 1982. The quotations were also selected by the author from *The Temple Shakespeare*, Cambridge edition (Dent, 1895).

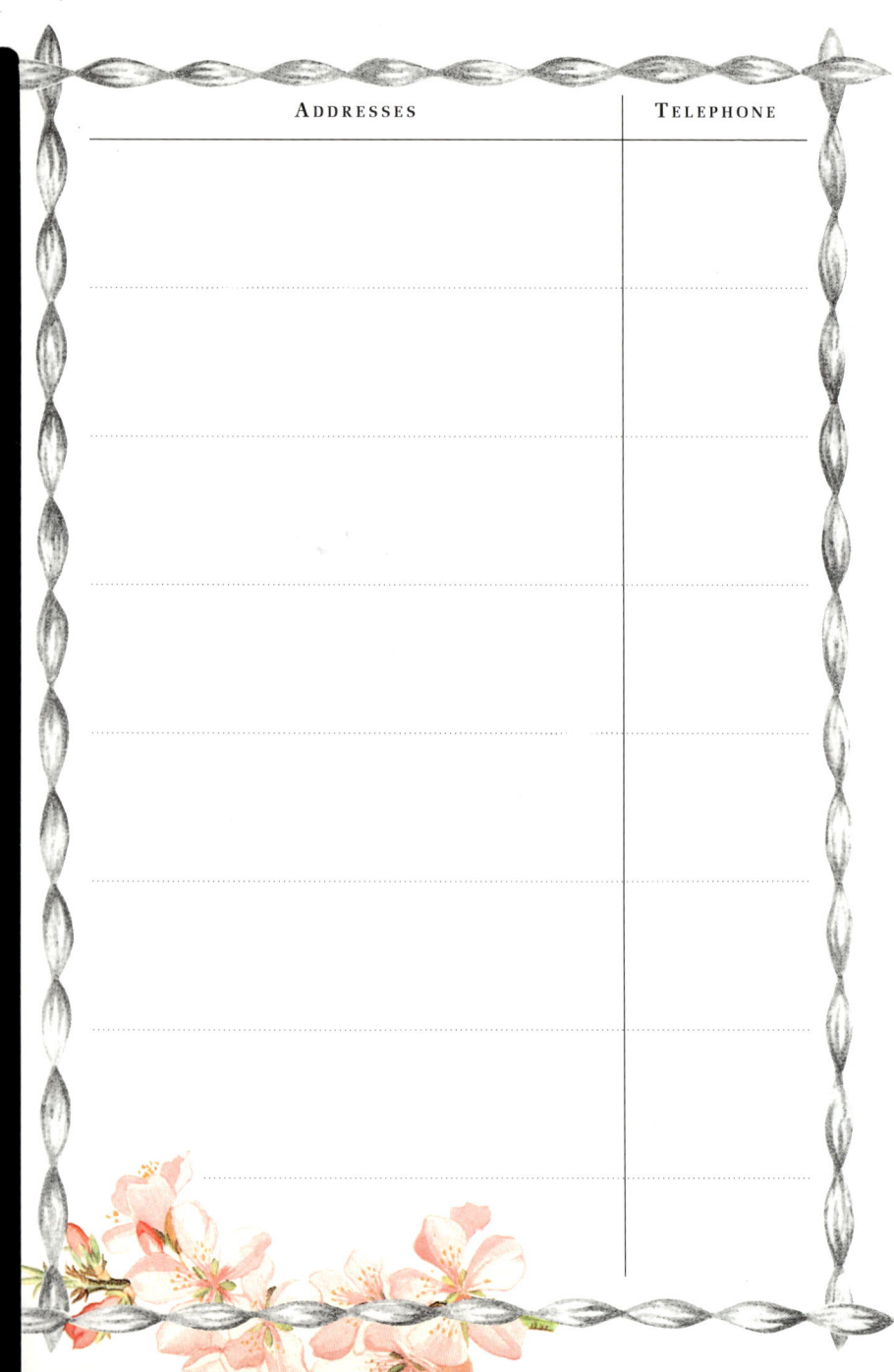

Addresses	Telephone

ADDRESSES | **TELEPHONE**

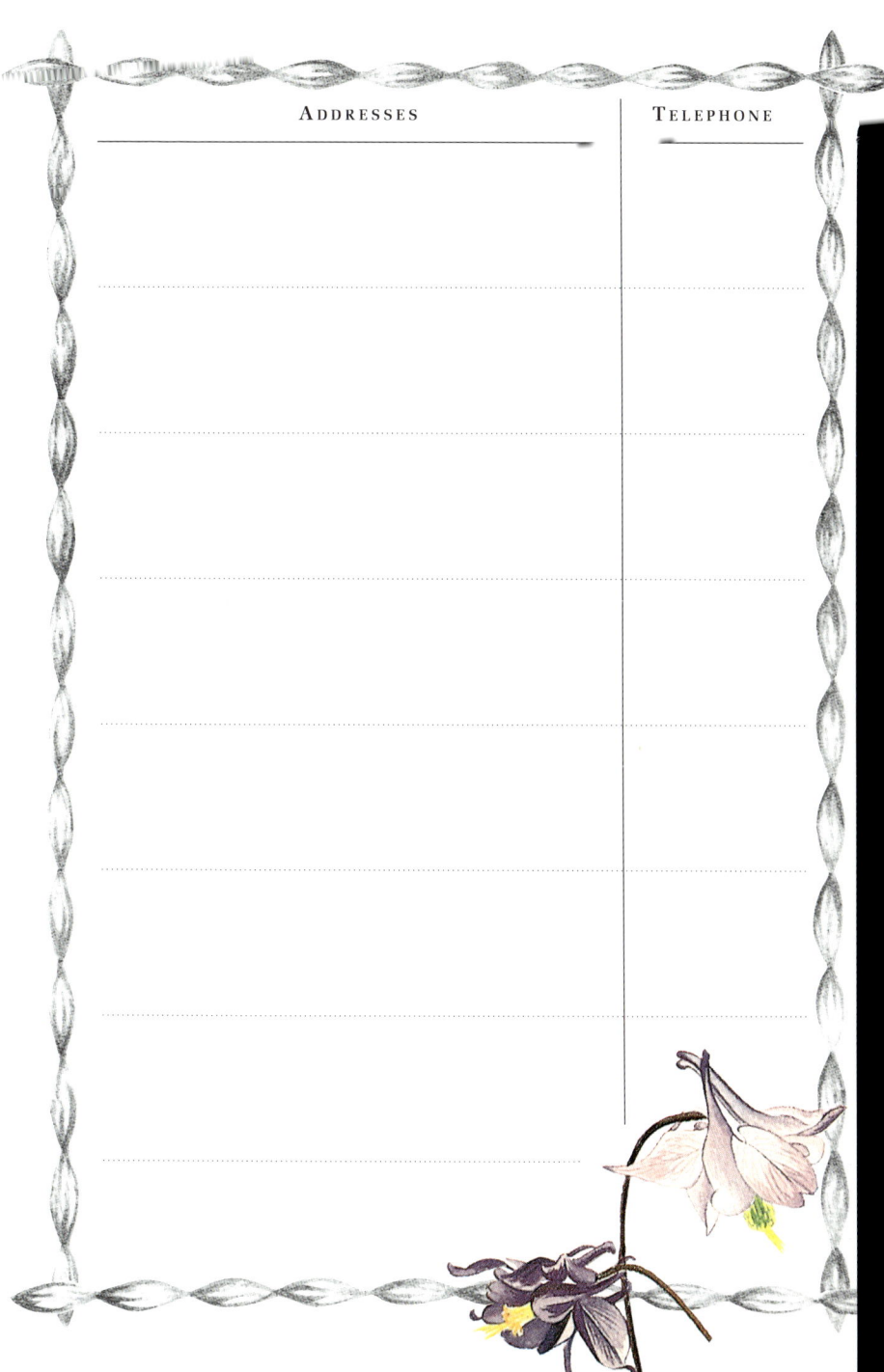

| Addresses | Telephone |

| **ADDRESSES** | **TELEPHONE** |

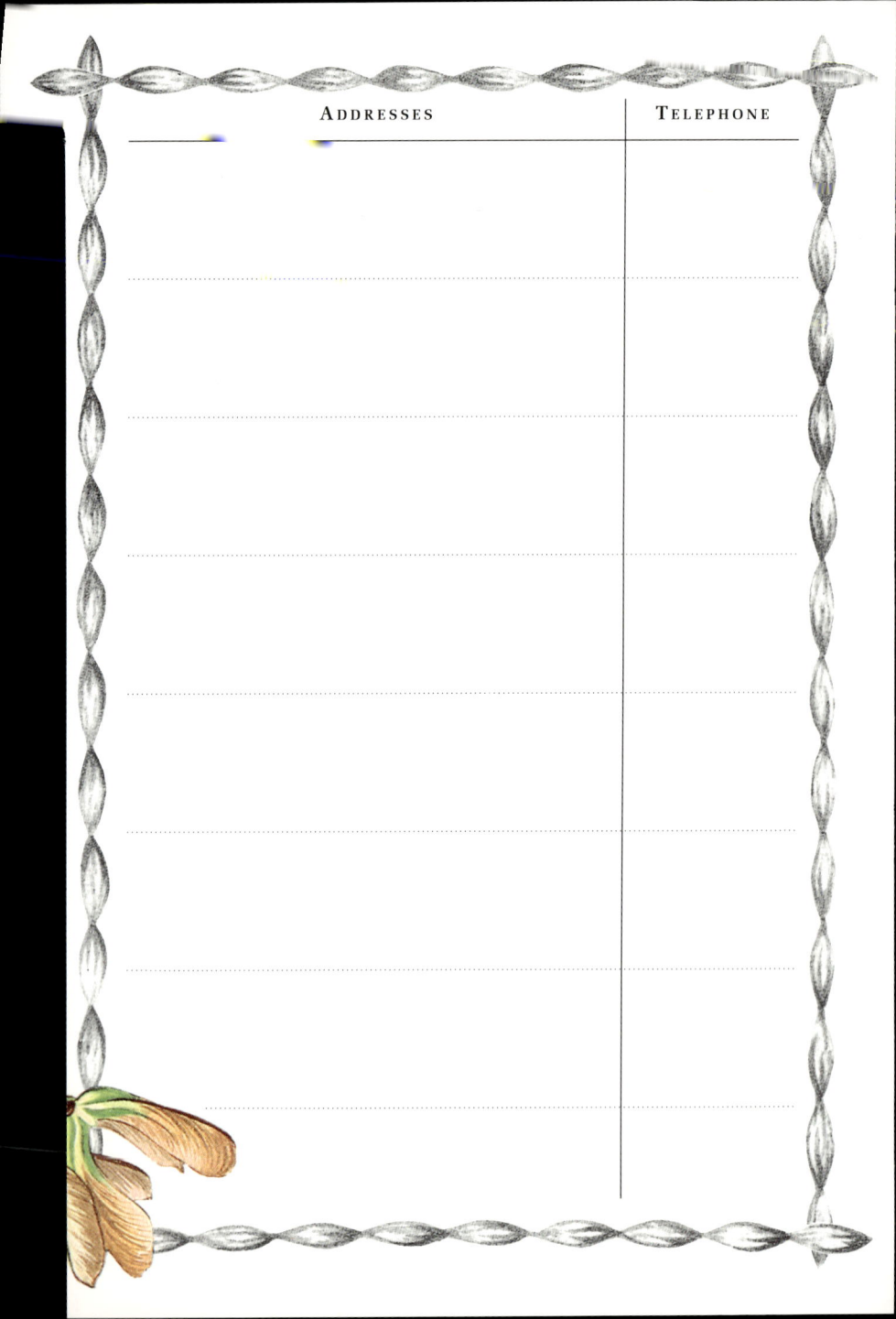

C

Addresses	Telephone

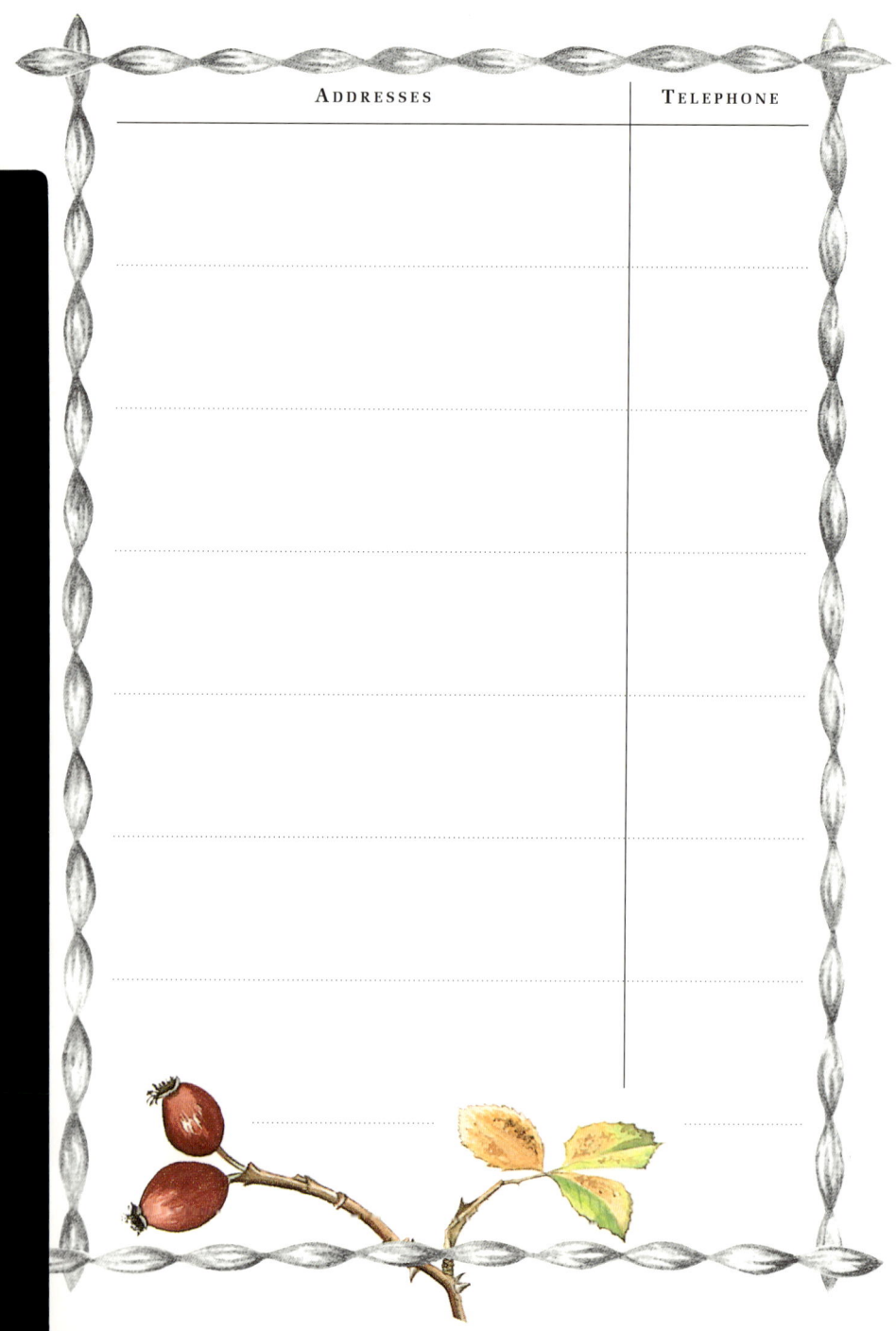

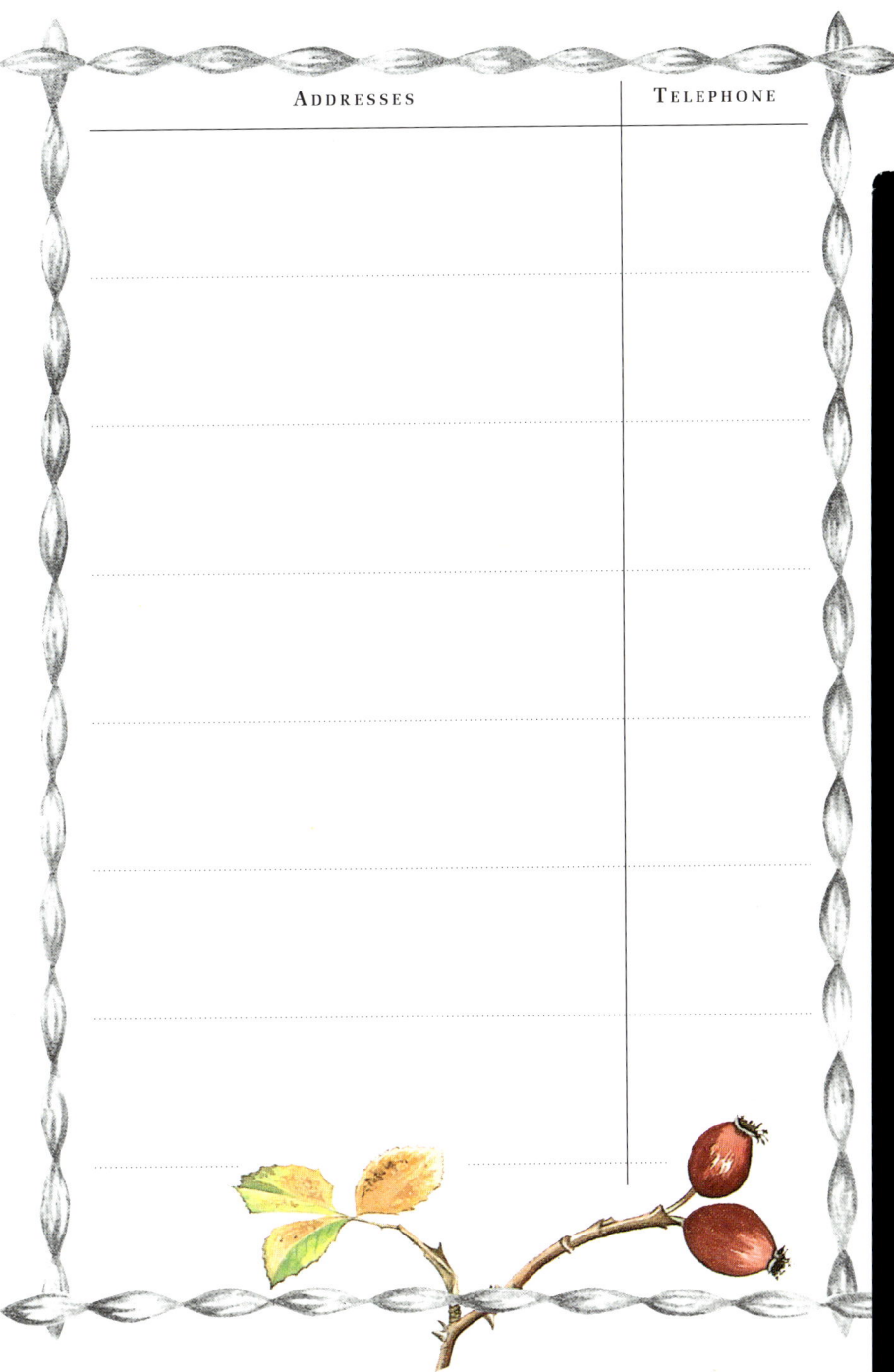

Addresses	Telephone

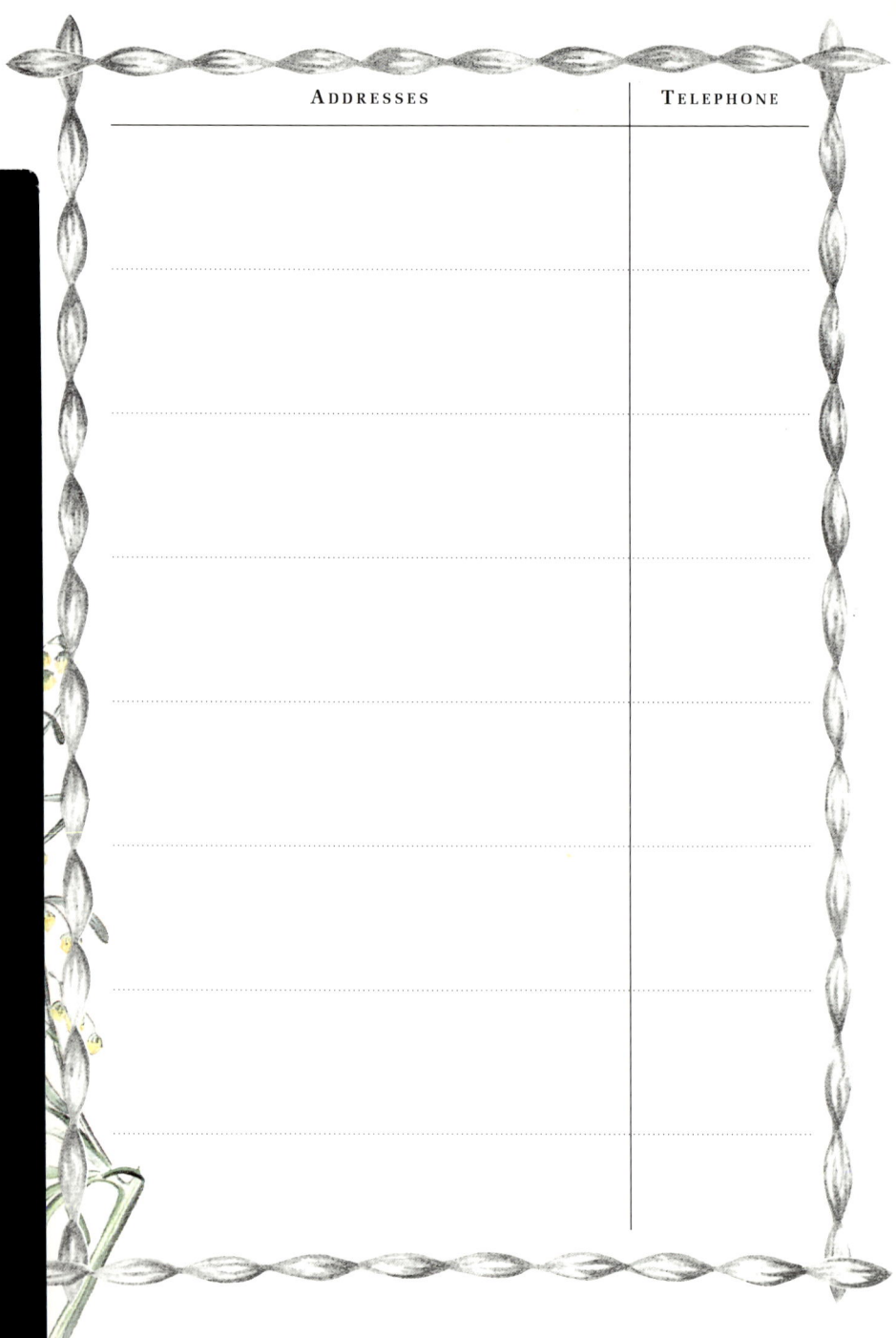

Addresses	Telephone

Addresses	Telephone

Addresses	Telephone

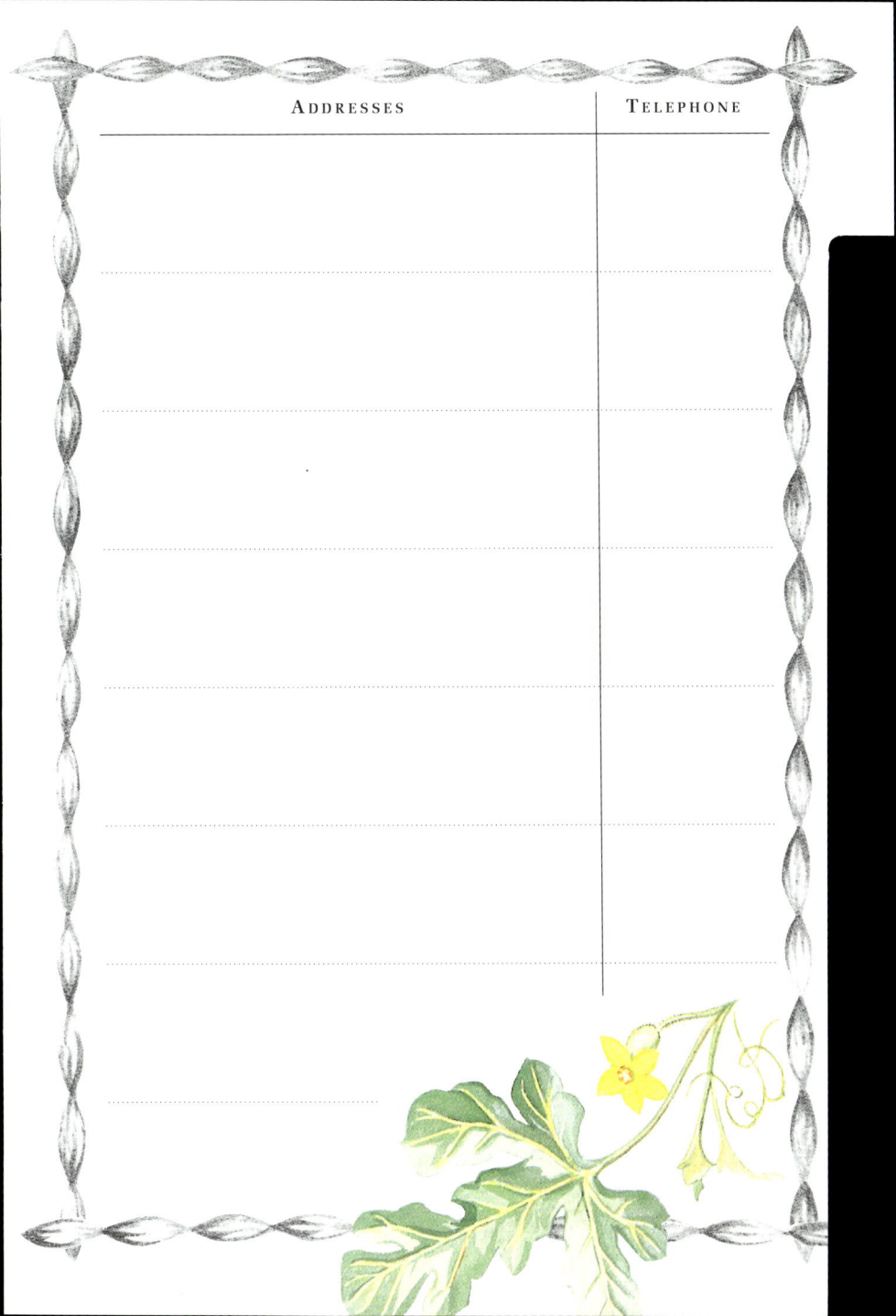

ADDRESSES	TELEPHONE

ADDRESSES	TELEPHONE

Addresses	Telephone

F

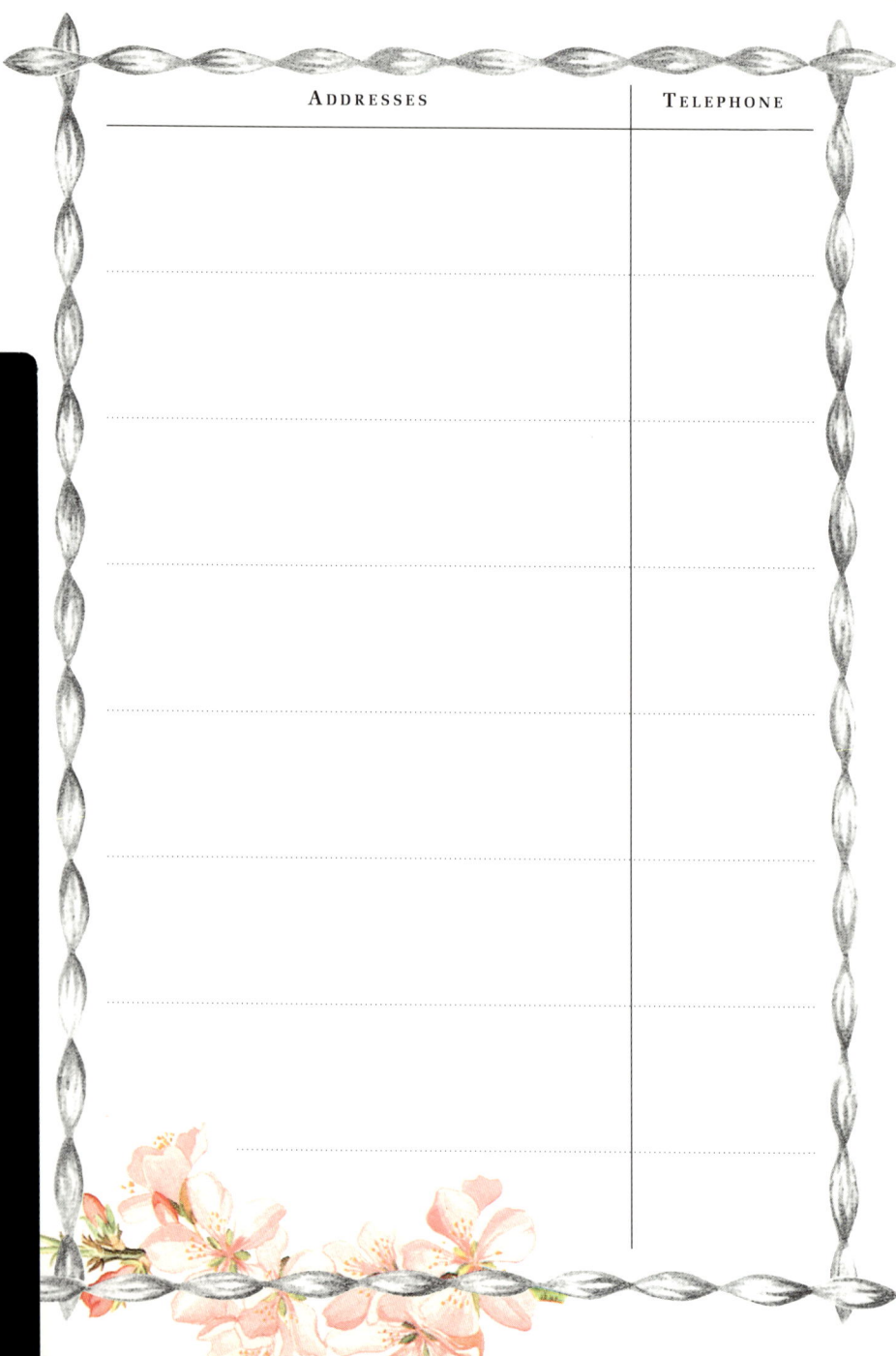

Addresses	Telephone

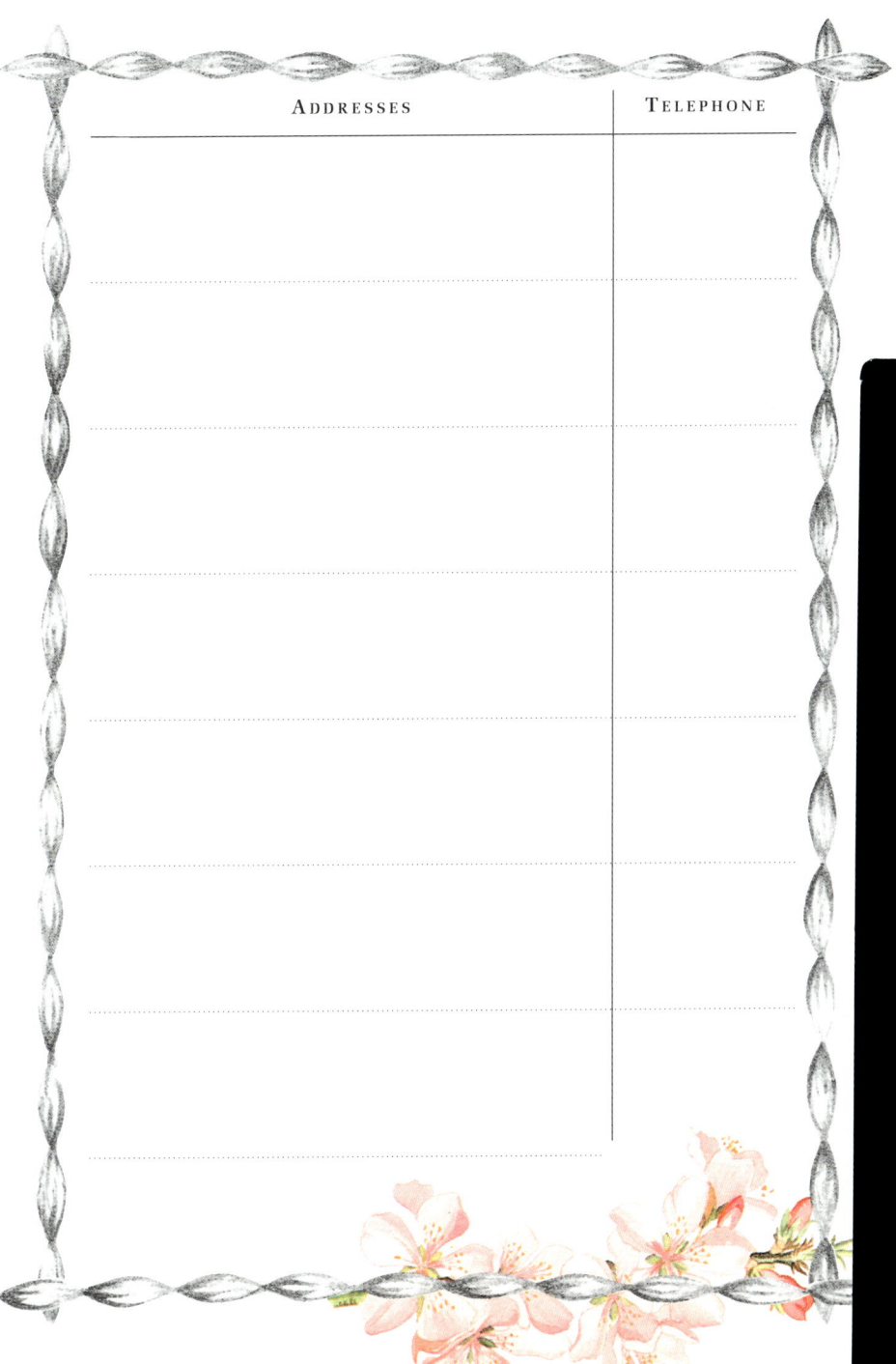

| Addresses | Telephone |

Addresses	Telephone

Addresses	Telephone

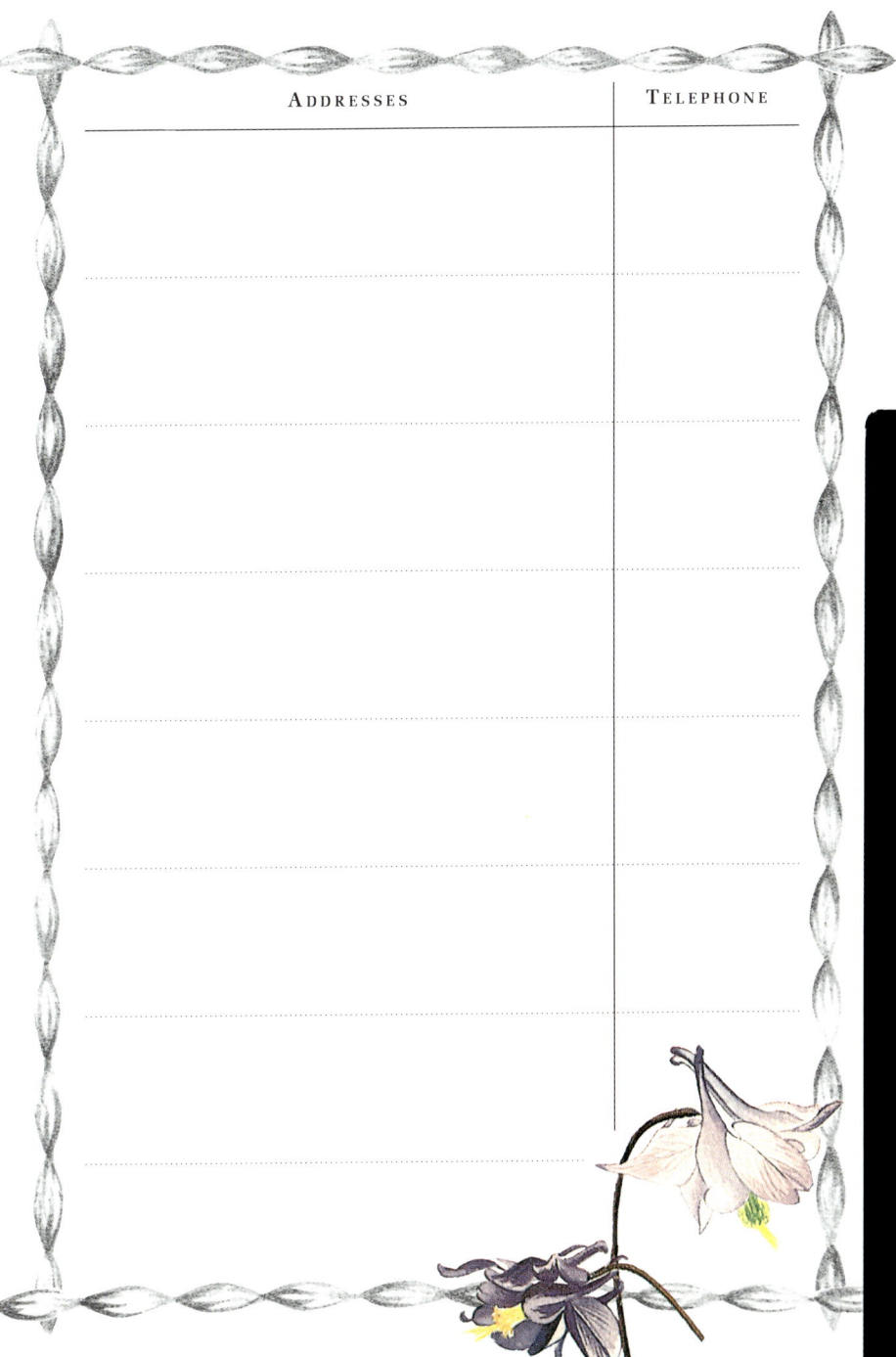

| Addresses | Telephone |

Addresses	Telephone

H

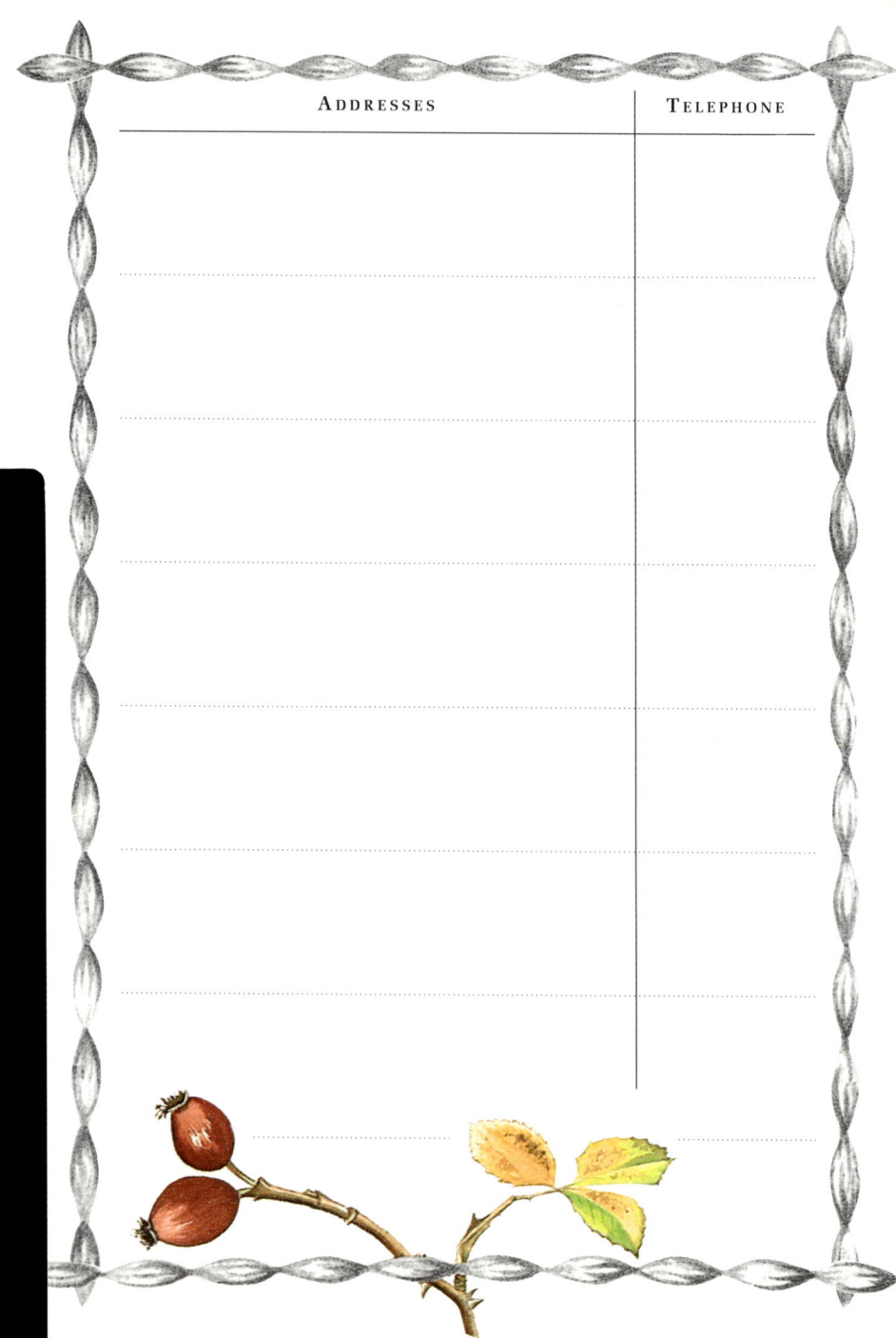

Addresses	Telephone

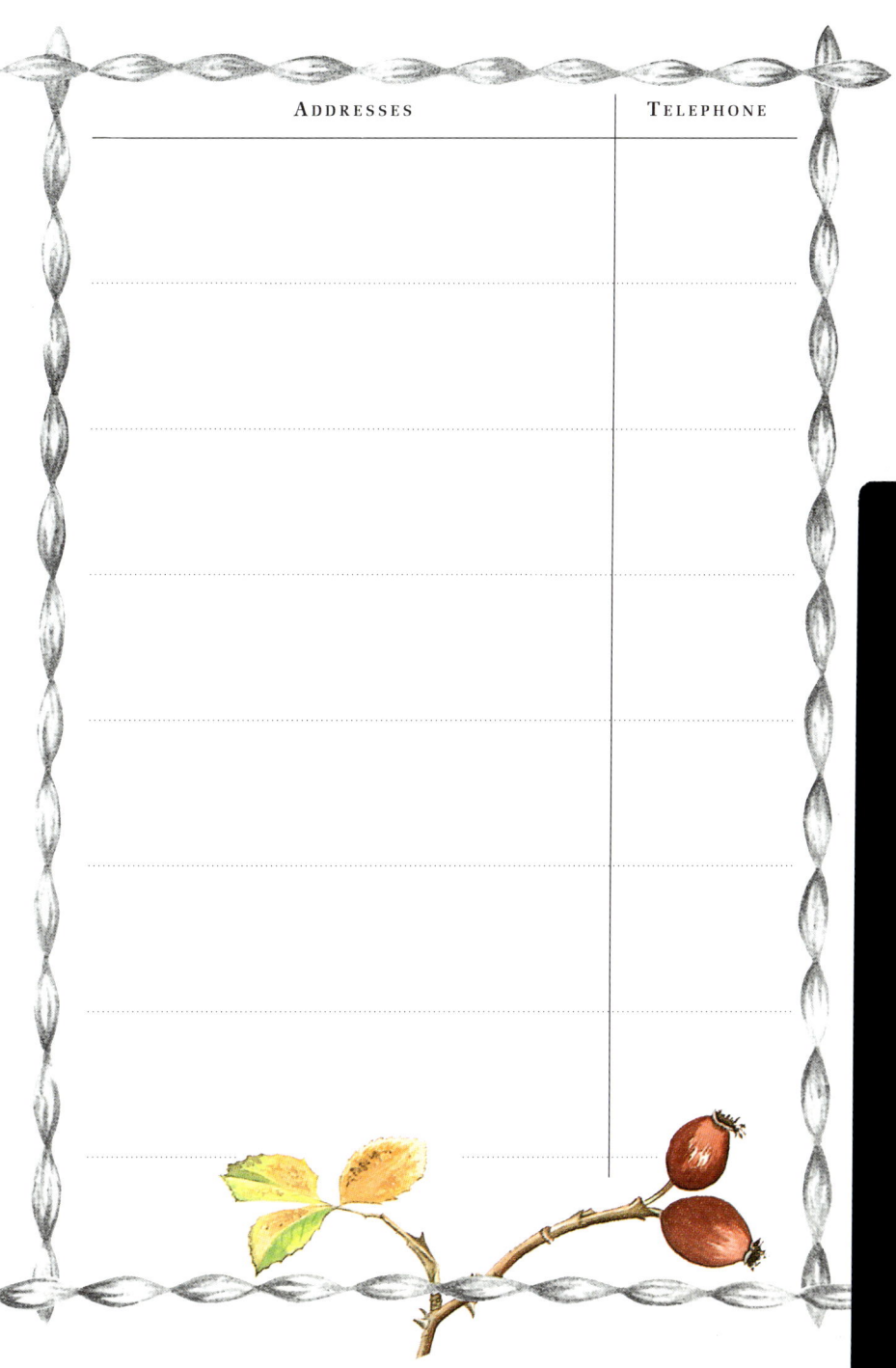

Addresses	Telephone

Addresses	Telephone

Addresses	Telephone

| Addresses | Telephone |

Addresses	Telephone

K

ADDRESSES	TELEPHONE

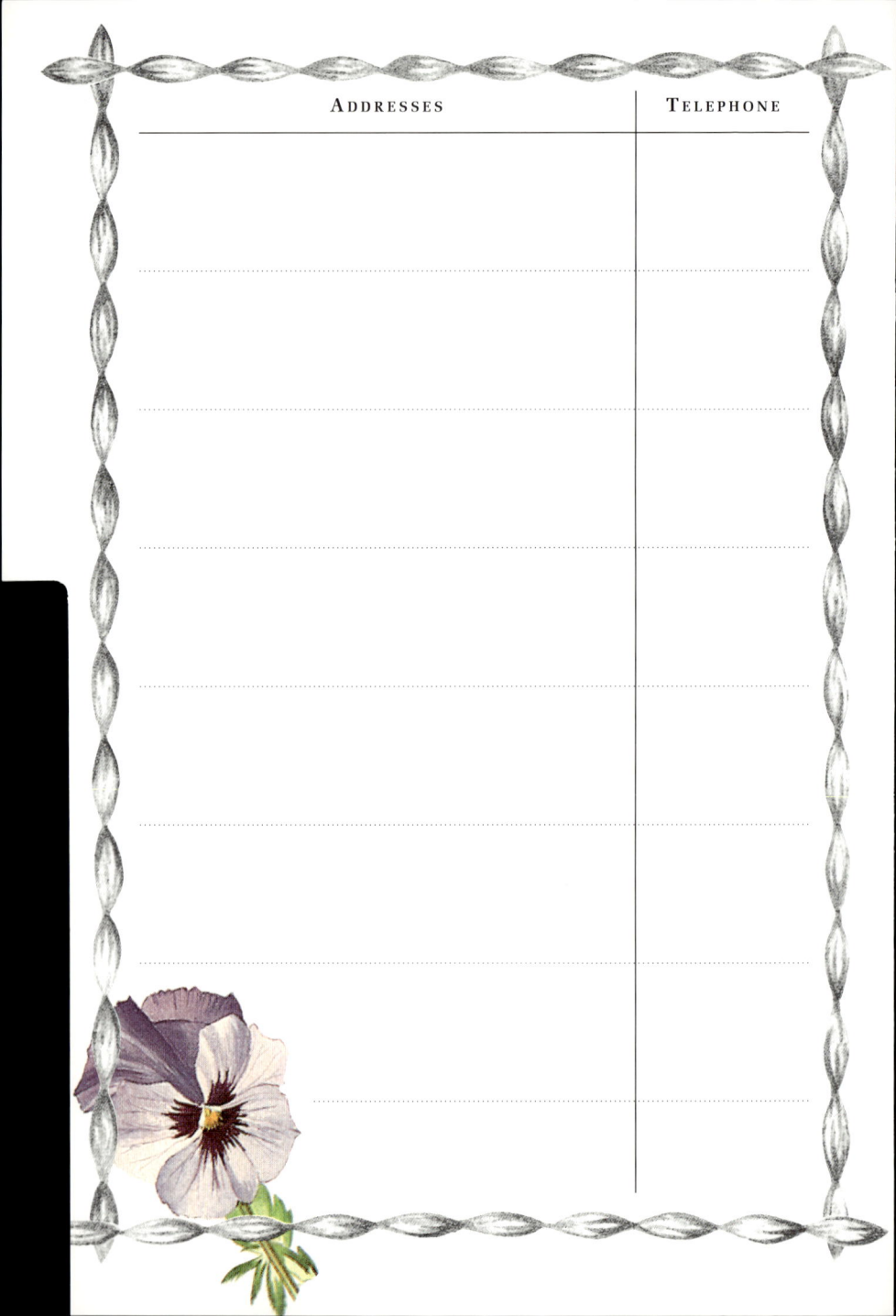

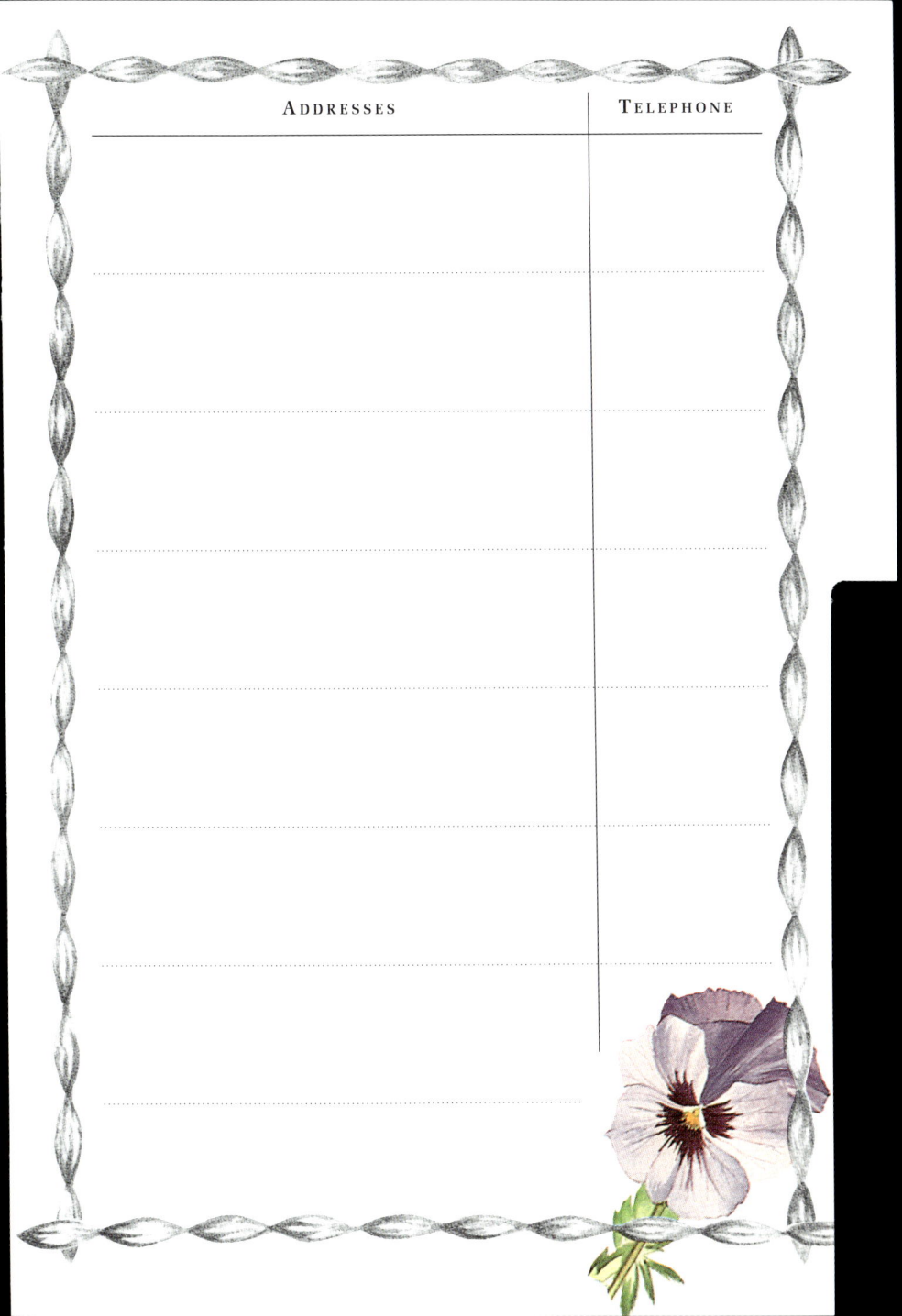

Addresses	Telephone

| ADDRESSES | TELEPHONE |

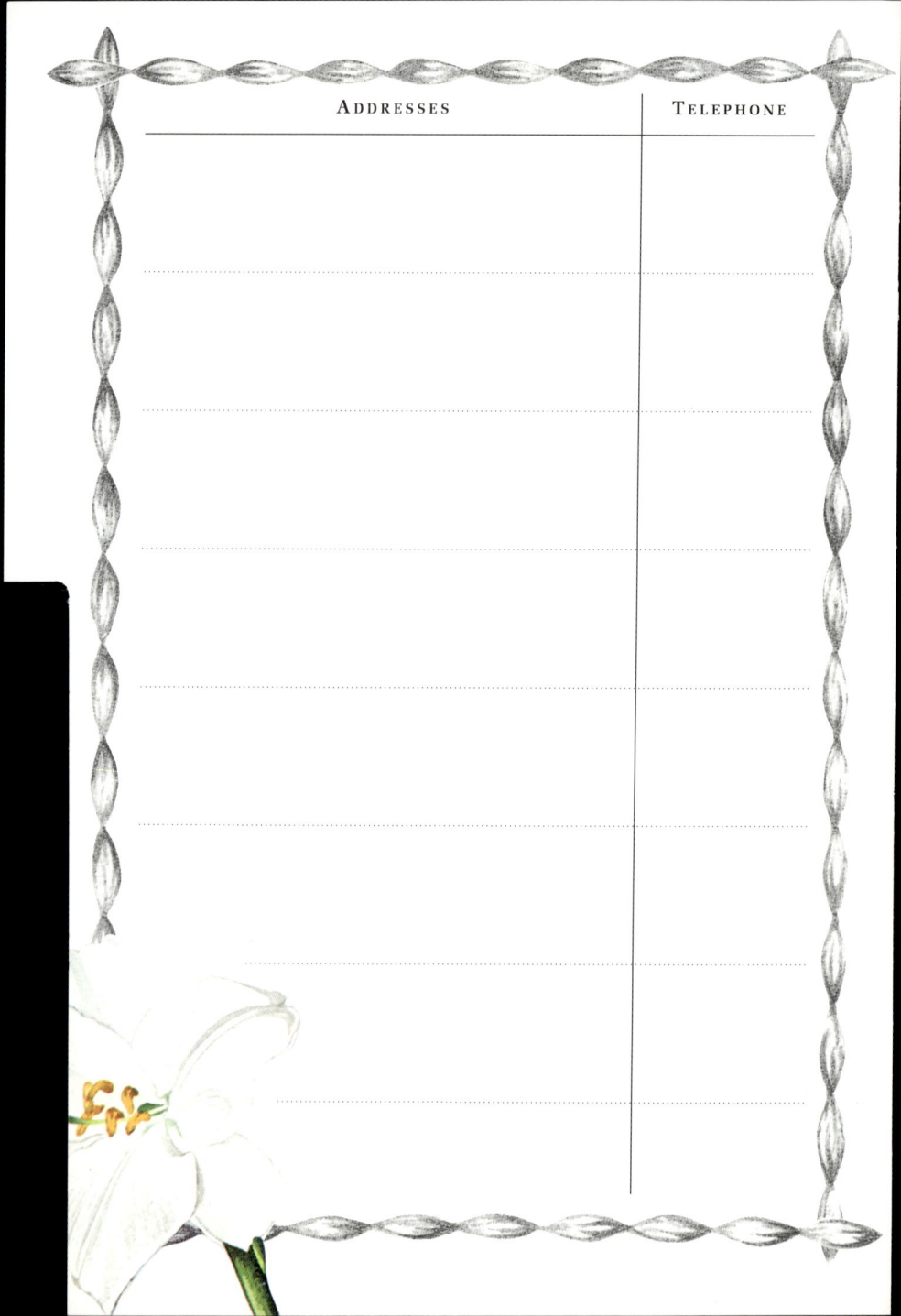

L

ADDRESSES	TELEPHONE

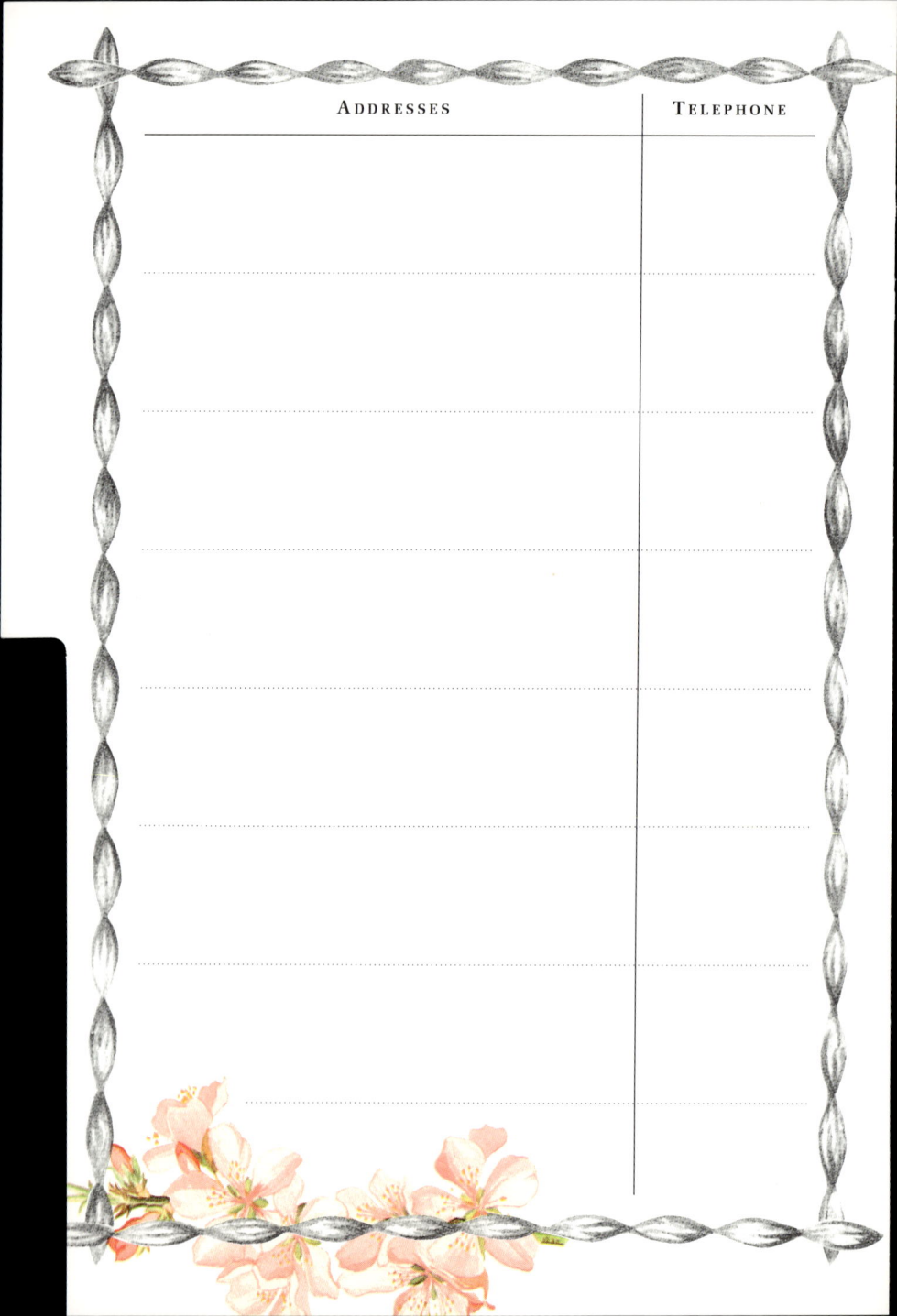

Addresses	Telephone

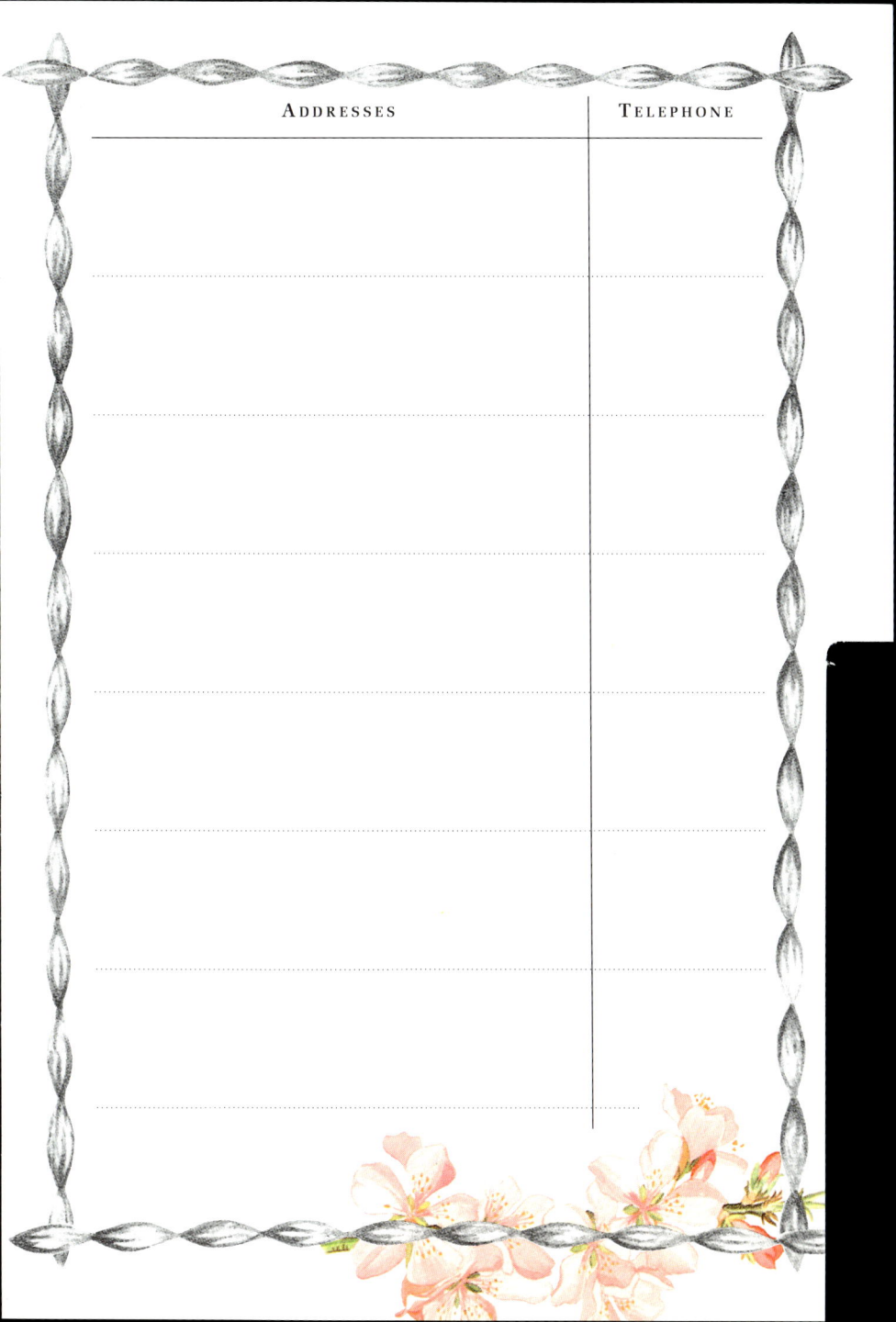

Addresses	Telephone

M

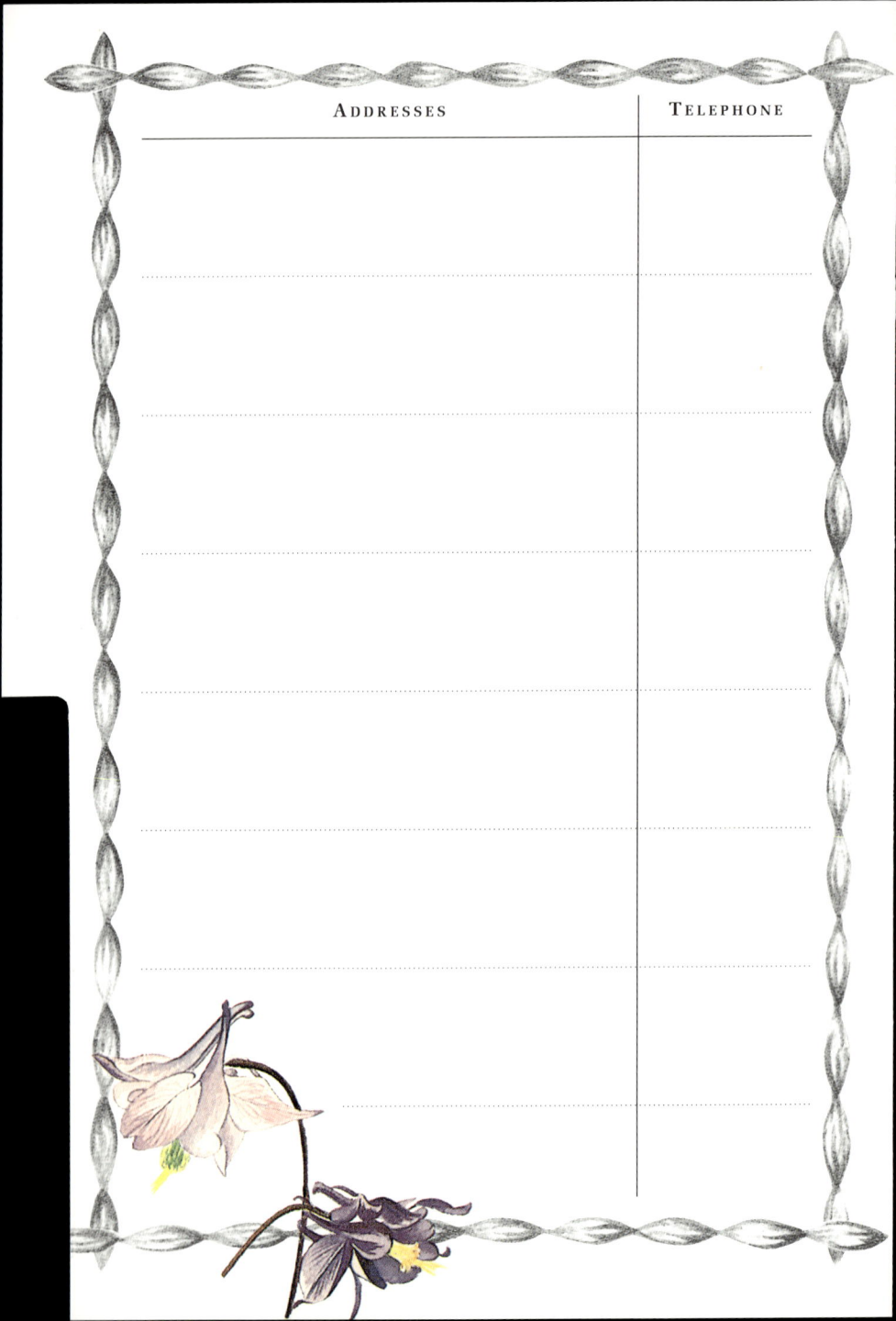

ADDRESSES	TELEPHONE

| Addresses | Telephone |

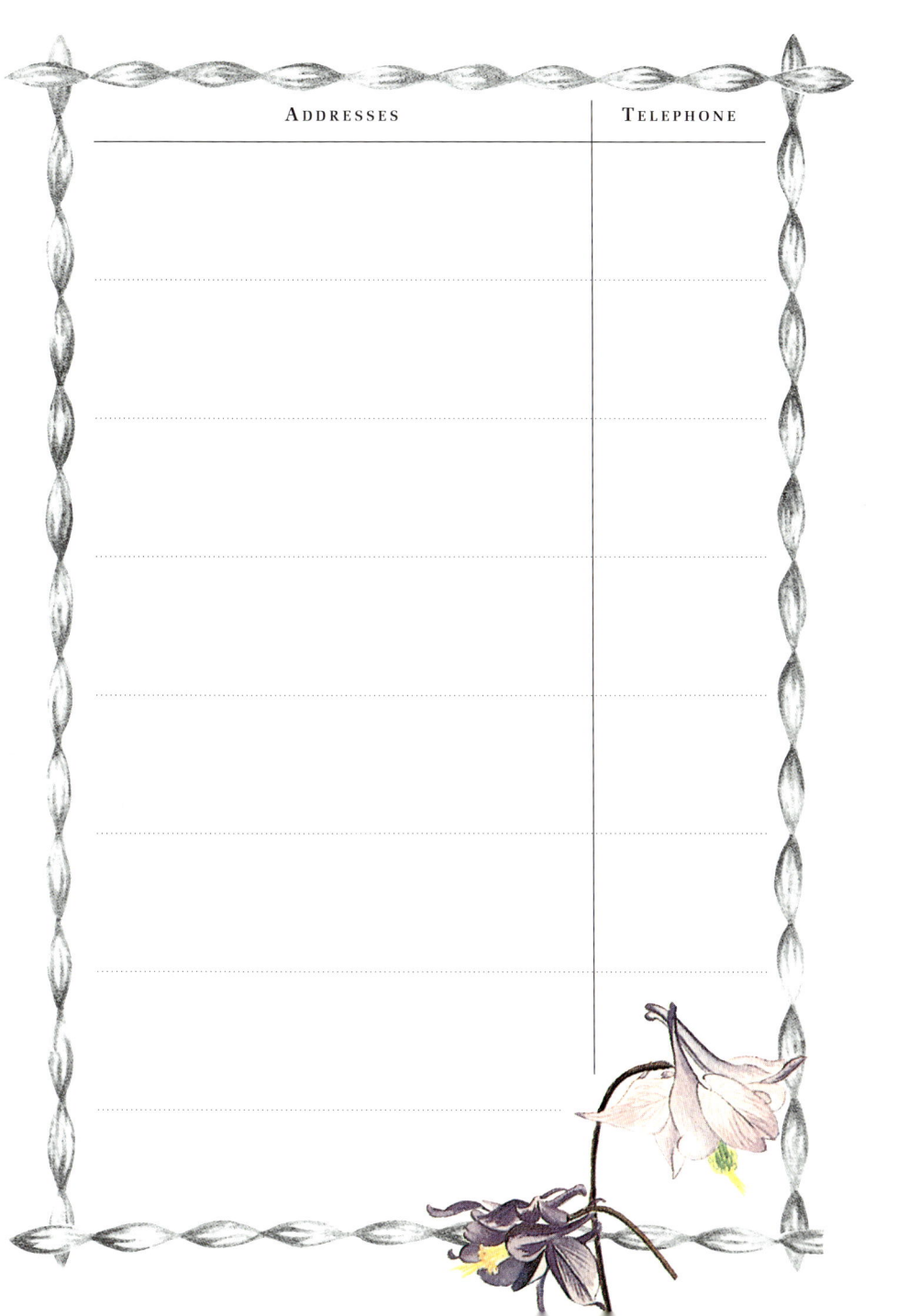

Addresses	Telephone

N

Addresses	Telephone

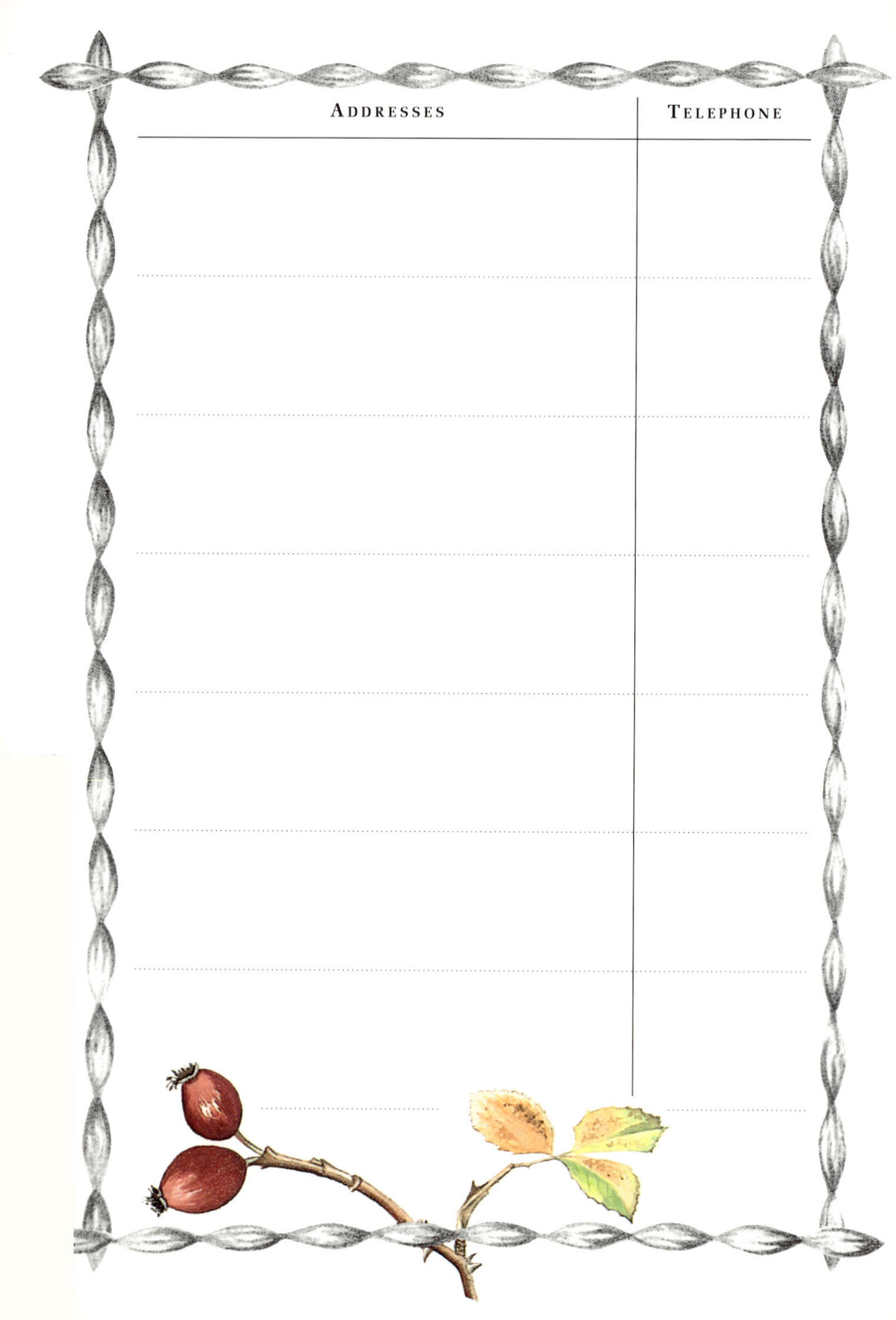

Addresses	Telephone

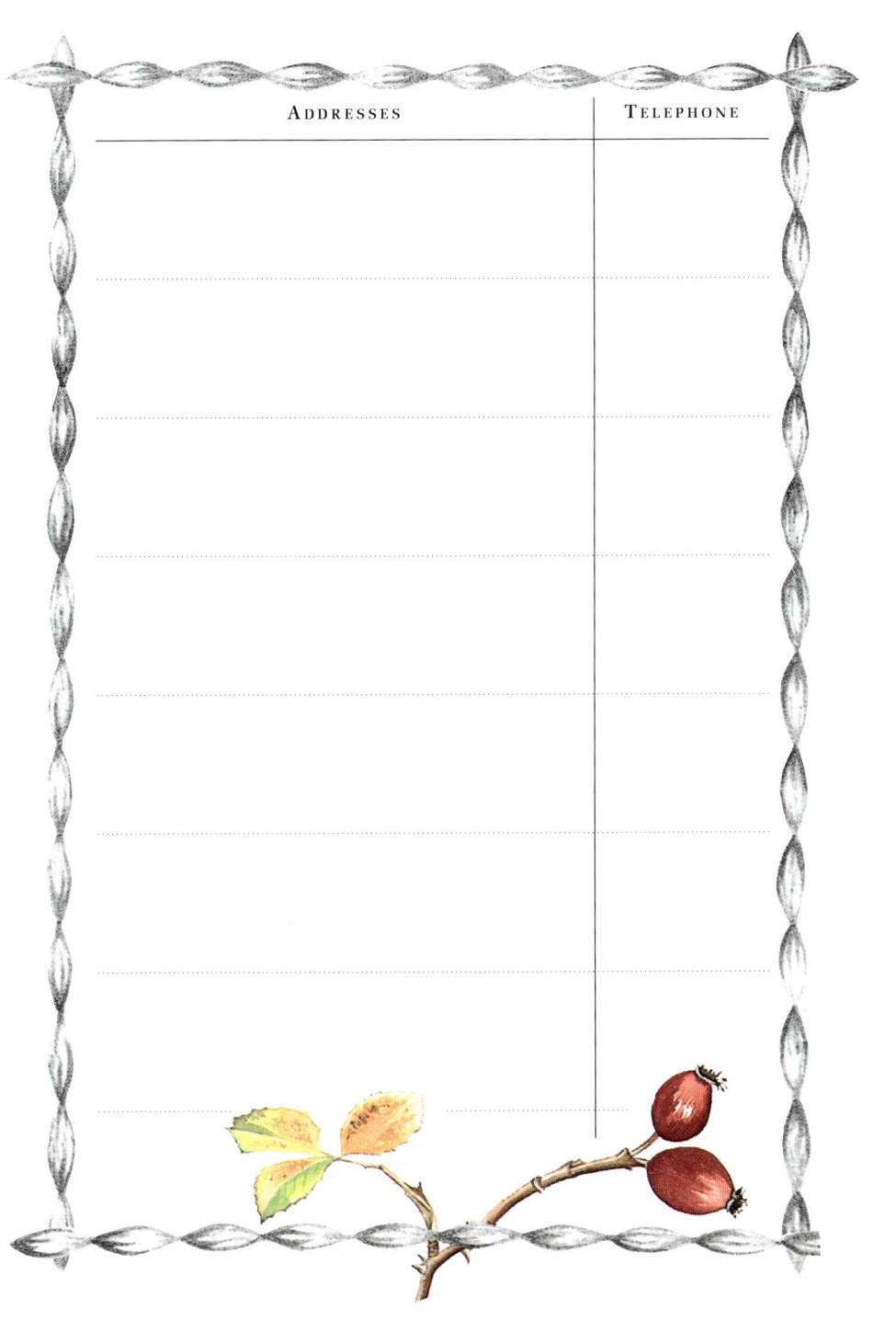

Addresses	Telephone

O

ADDRESSES	TELEPHONE

Addresses	Telephone

Addresses	Telephone

P

Addresses	Telephone

Addresses	Telephone

Addresses	Telephone

Q

Addresses	Telephone

Addresses	Telephone

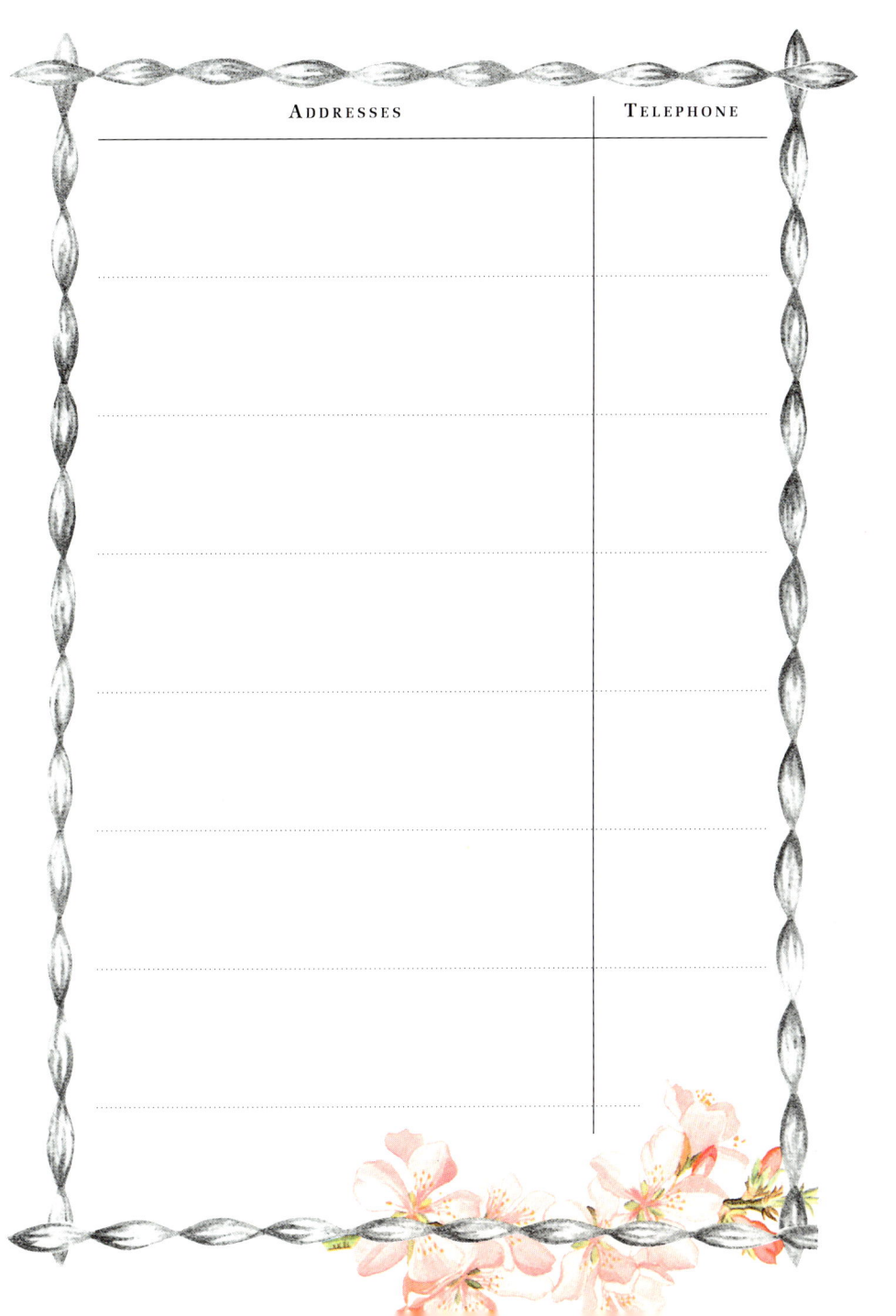

ADDRESSES	TELEPHONE

R

ADDRESSES	TELEPHONE

Addresses	Telephone

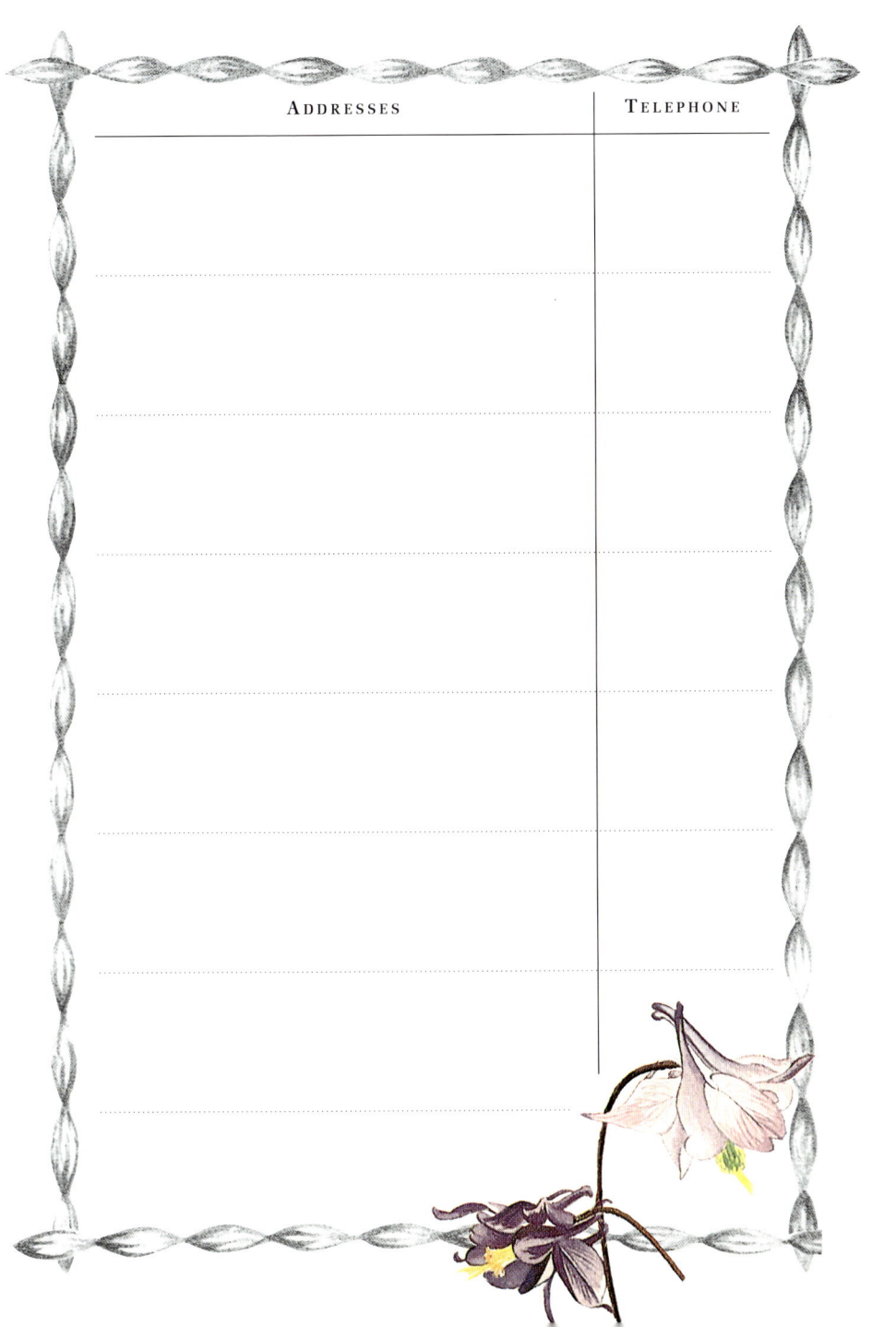

Addresses	Telephone

S

ADDRESSES	TELEPHONE

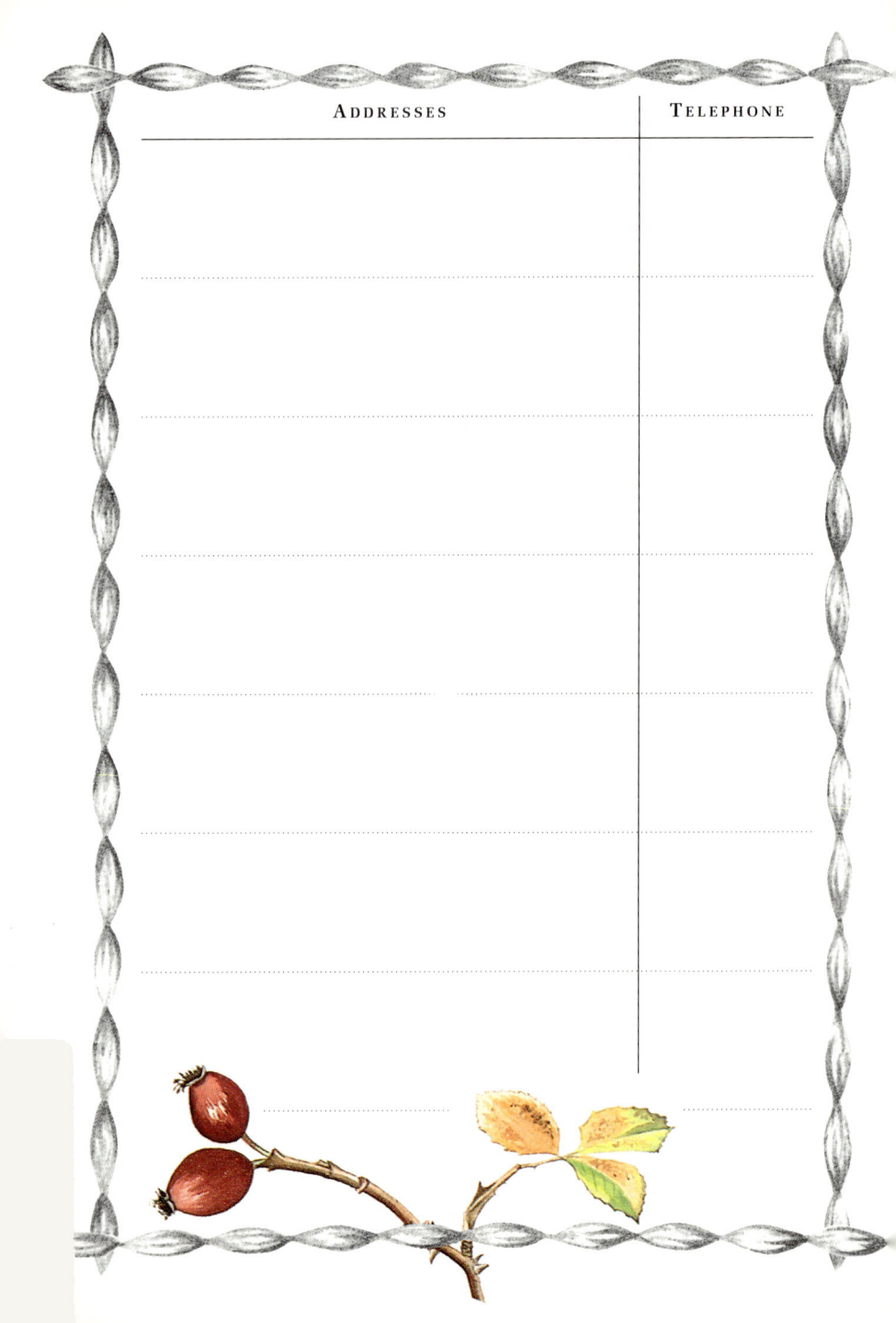

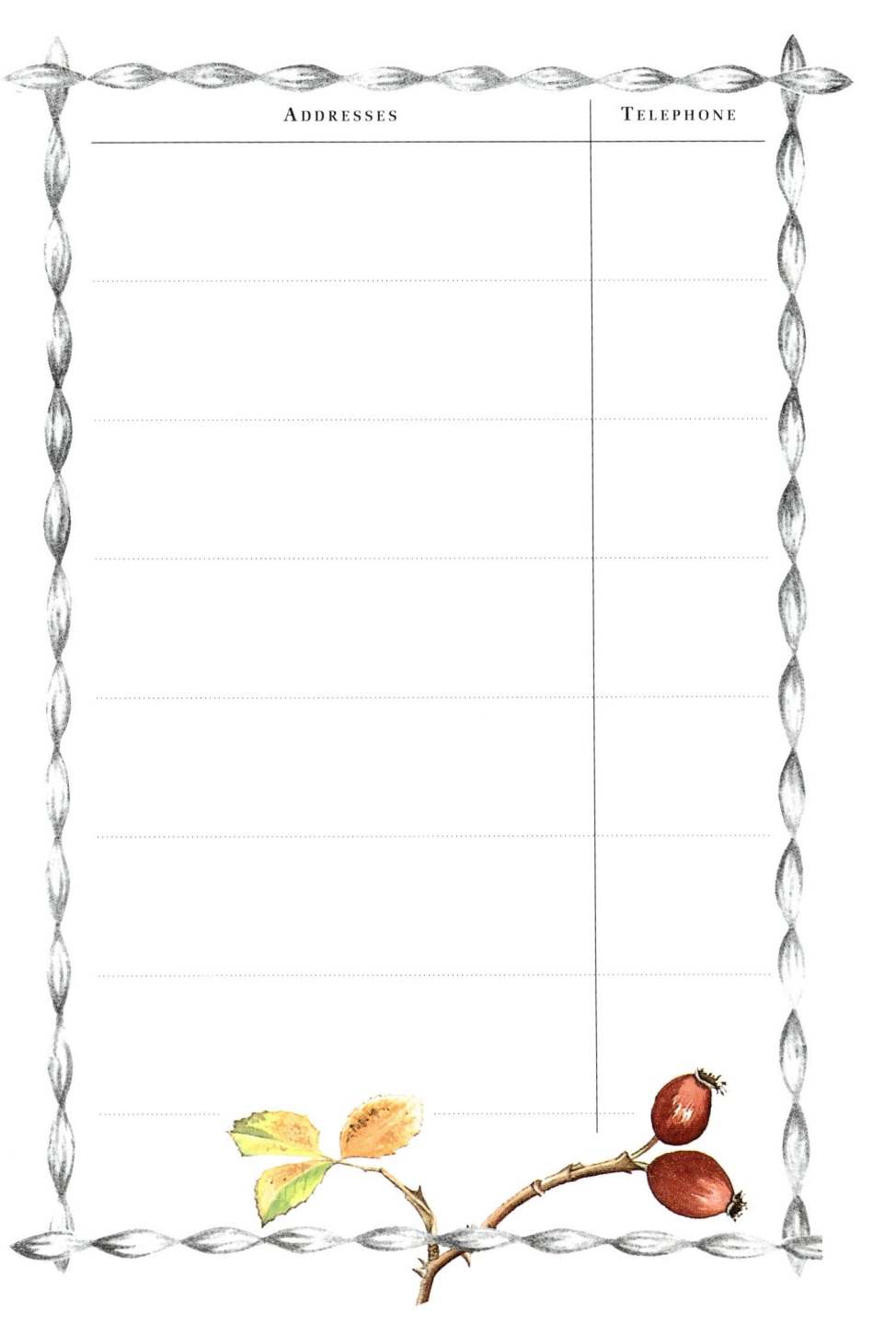

Addresses	Telephone

| ADDRESSES | TELEPHONE |

T

Addresses	Telephone

ADDRESSES	TELEPHONE

ADDRESSES	TELEPHONE

U

ADDRESSES	TELEPHONE

Addresses	Telephone

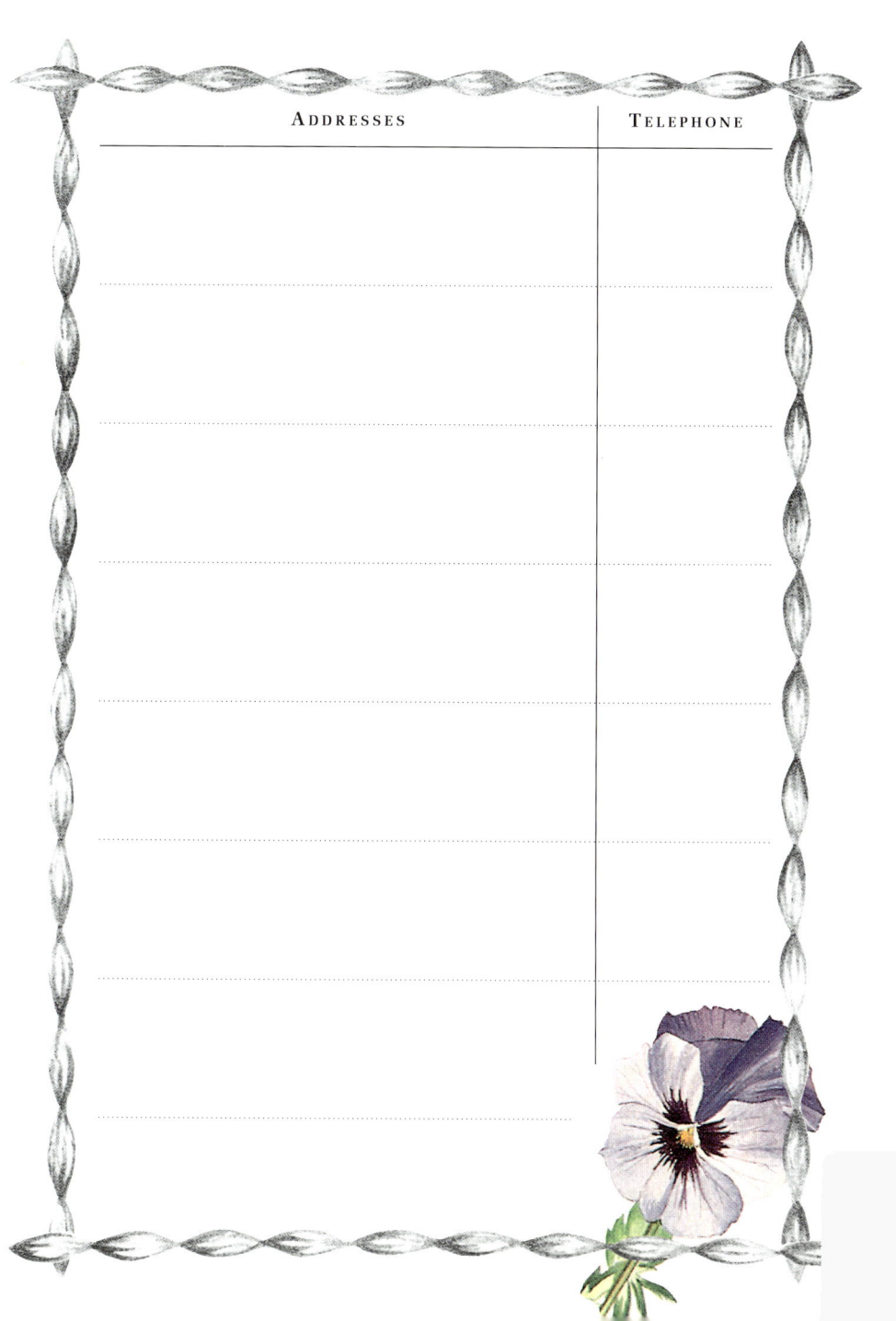

Addresses	Telephone

VW

Addresses	Telephone

Addresses	Telephone

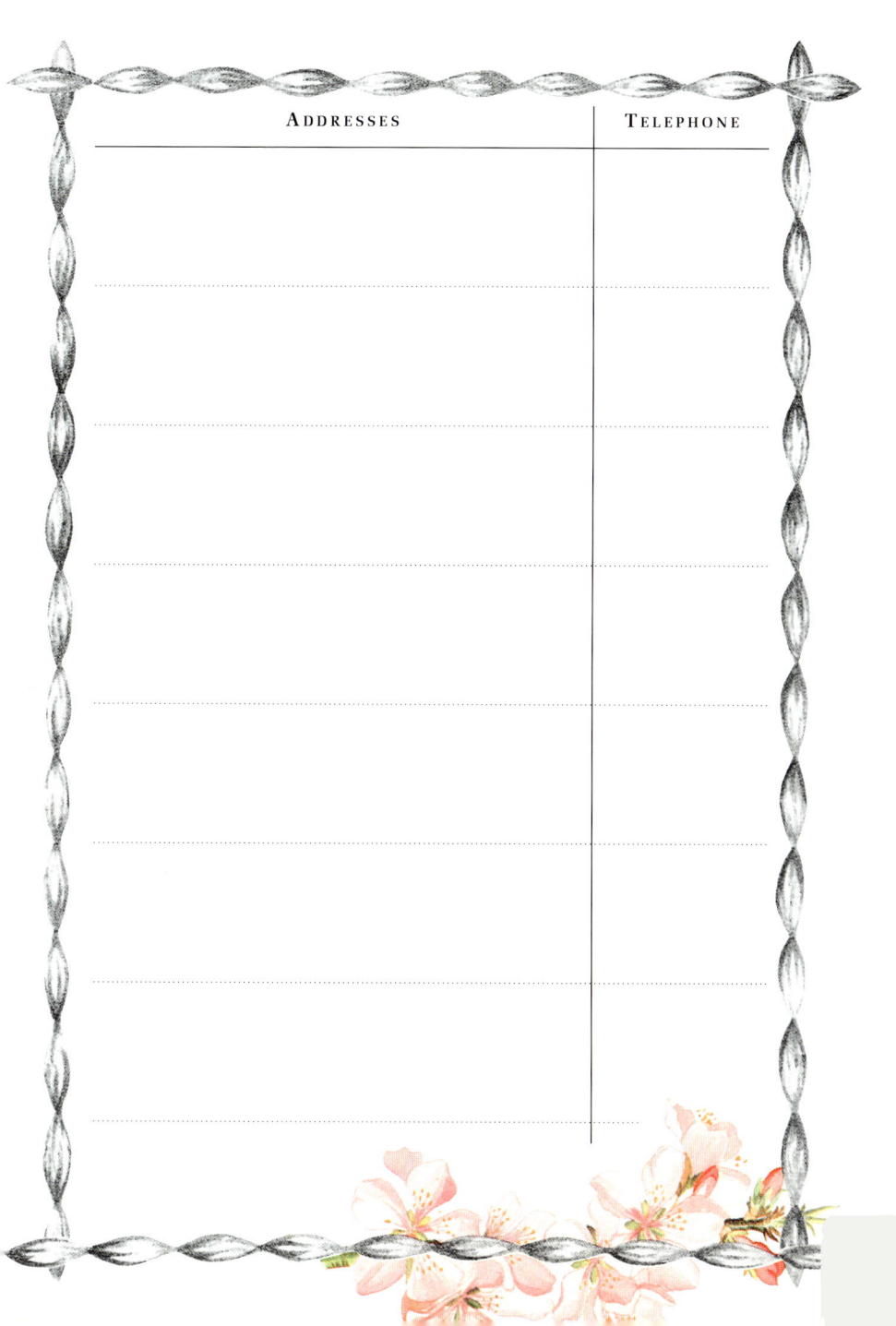

Addresses	Telephone

XY

ADDRESSES	TELEPHONE

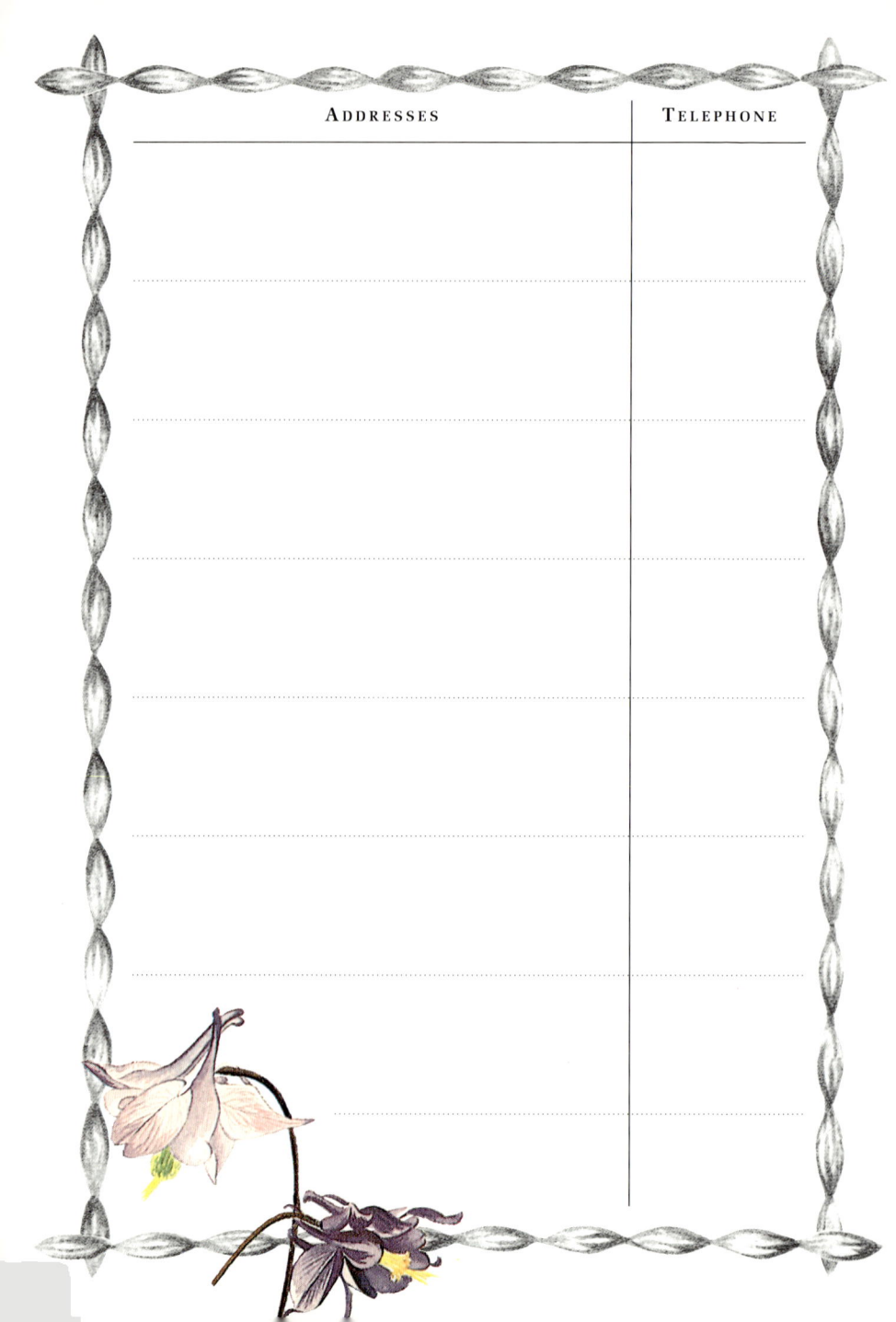

Addresses	Telephone

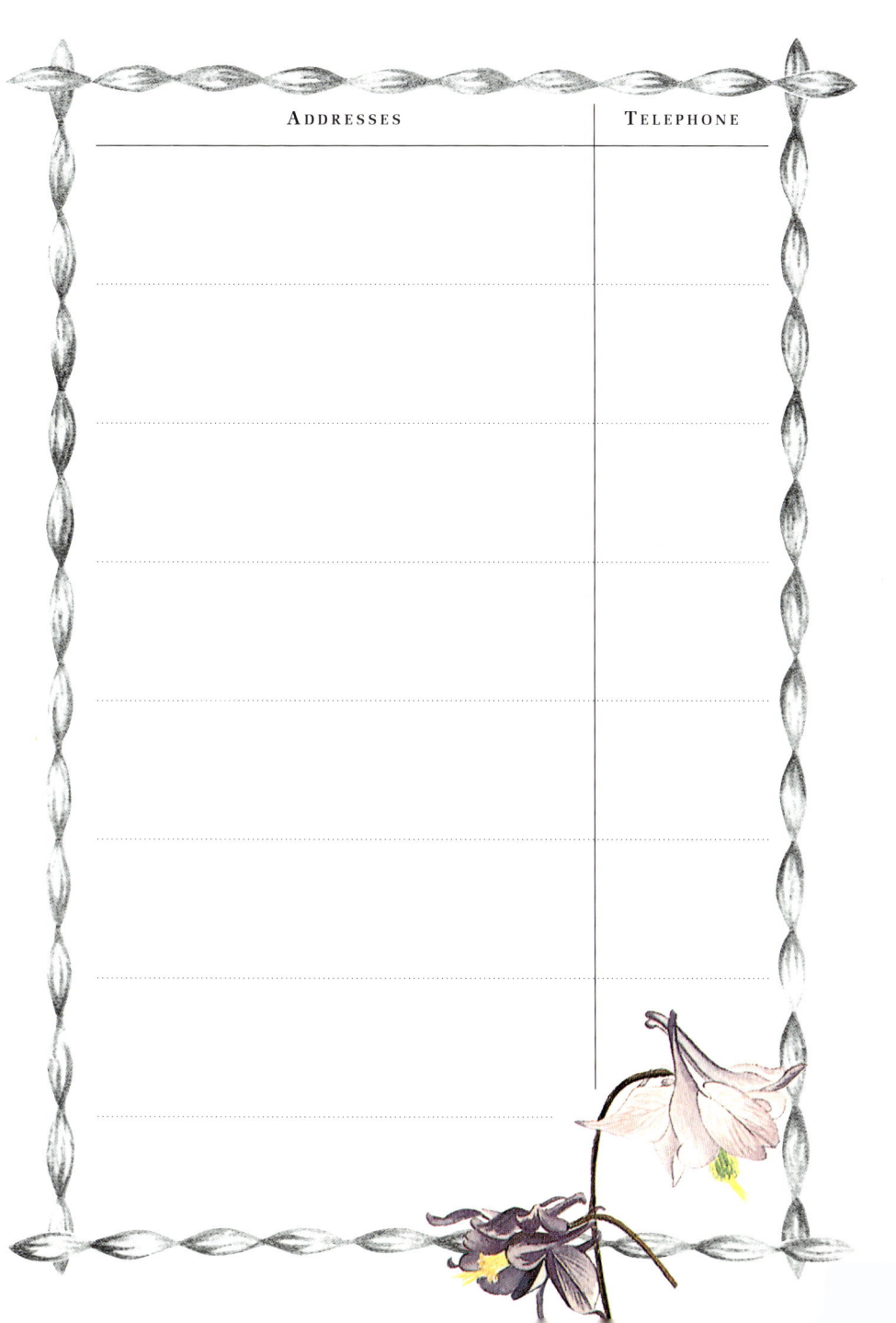

Addresses	Telephone

Z

Addresses	Telephone

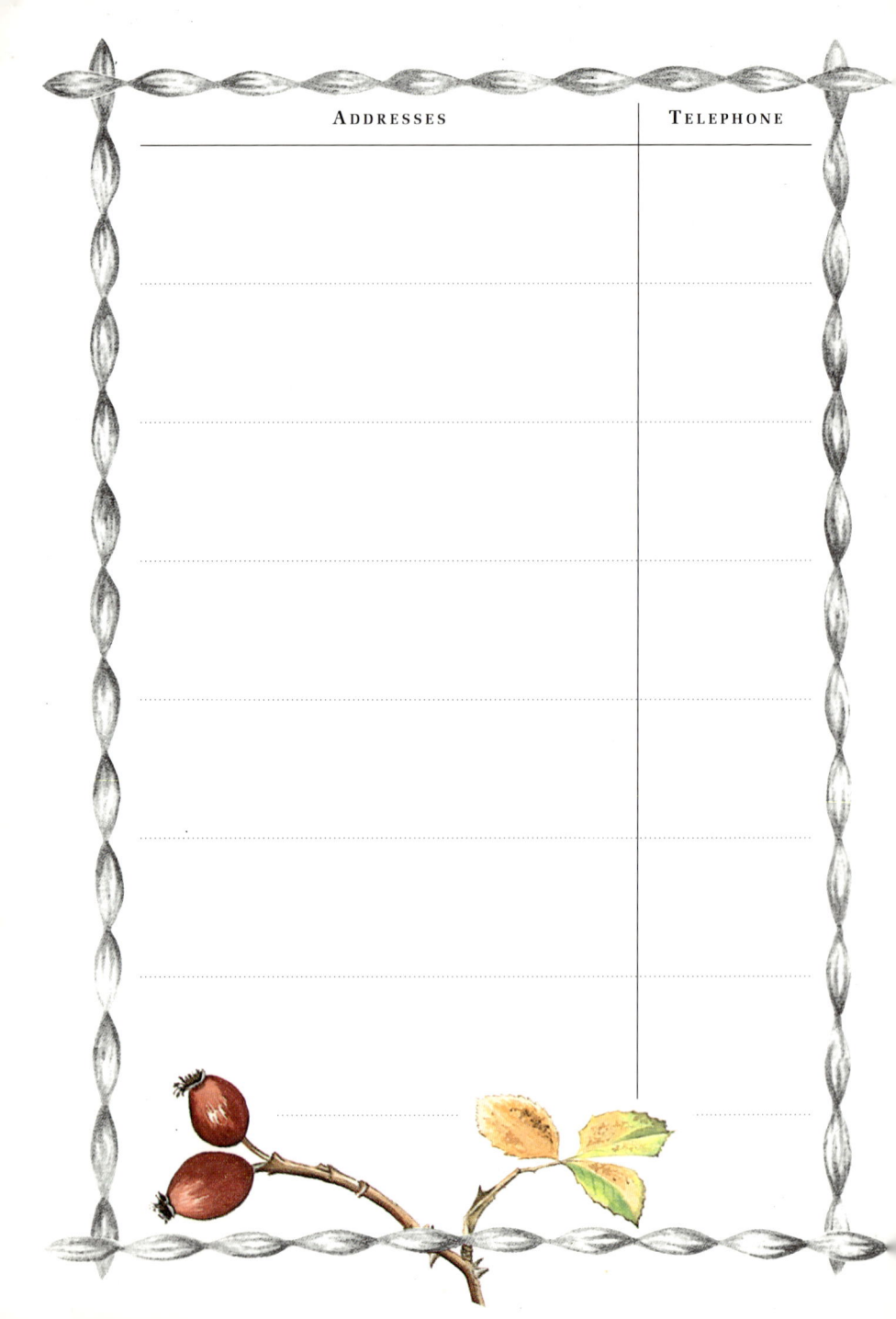